# CLASSIC
# CARS
## FROM AROUND THE WORLD

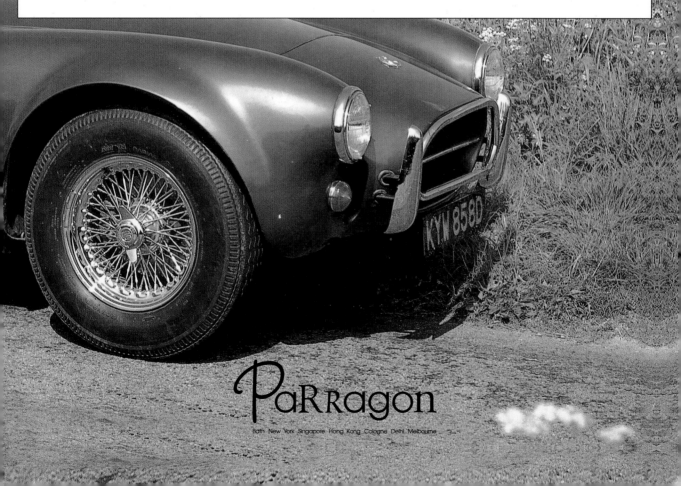

# CLASSIC
# CARS
## FROM AROUND THE WORLD

MICHAEL BOWLER

PaRRagon

Bath New York Singapore Hong Kong Cologne Delhi Melbourne

*Page 1*
*The beautiful Dino 246GT was*
*not stictly a Ferrari, but was*
*intended to establish a new sub-*
*Ferrari marque; its successor was*
*eventually promoted to full*
*Maranello status.*

*Pages 2-3*
*The AC Cobra 289 is the most*
*copied classic of all-time, a*
*tribute to the style of the original*
*Ace of 13 years earlier than this*
*1966 version.*

This edition published by Parragon in 2009

Parragon
Queen Street House
4 Queen Street
Bath BA1 1HE, UK

Copyright © Parragon Books Ltd 1999
Designed and produced by
Stonecastle Graphics Limited

ISBN 978-1-4075-7712-8
Printed in Indonesia

Photography credits

All photographs by Neill Bruce Motoring
Photolibrary with the exception of the following:
*(Abbreviations: r=right, l=left, t=top, b=below)*
The Peter Roberts Collection: pages 13(b), 21, 24,
31(t), 41(t), 51(b), 64, 73(t), 73(b), 81(t), 81(b), 88,
92, 93(b).
Andrew Morland: pages 22, 23(b), 30, 53(r), 55(t),
70, 72, 77(t), 83(b), 84, 90, 91(b).
The National Motor Museum, Beaulieu, England:
pages 20(b), 29(b), 32(l) *Nicky Wright*, 44, 45(t) *Nicky
wright*, 62-63, 74 *Nicky Wright*, 75(b) *Nicky Wright*,
82 *Nicky Wright*, 87(t), 87(b).
David Hotges: pages 25(t), 29(t), 40-41(b), 83(t), 86.
Bengt Holm: page 39(r).
Michael Bowler: page 43(b).
Front cover image: 1952 Jaguar C-Type © Getty Images

With grateful thanks to Neill Bruce for his kind
assistance and patience, and to the other
photographers and copyright holders for their
contributions.

# CONTENTS

*Left: The classically stylish Ferrari 275 GTB; this is a 1965 'short-nose'.*

# INTRODUCTION

Classic is one of those terms that every like-minded enthusiast understands but few can define to the satisfaction of all. In broad terms it seems to apply to any obsolete car for which there are sufficient enthusiasts to form a car club, but the ability of a handful of cars to survive the ravages of time and rust should not automatically make them classics; if they were regarded as unimpressive in their day, they don't get better. So today's classic car should have been at least a little out of the ordinary in its day, even if it's only the top of an otherwise mundane range – the Cortina GT might qualify but everyman's Cortina 1200 shouldn't.

Outside the USA, Classic has become the catch-all term for anything that seems to be old and well looked after, and it also embraces periods for which there are established definitions. Within the USA there is a nation-wide Classic Car Club which caters for carefully selected grander cars from the 1925-42 period plus a few younger ones of particular merit. Around most of the rest of the world the definitions have stemmed from the great British obsession with the older car – the International body FIVA has endorsed their years of change if not necessarily their names.

The oldest have been called Veterans since the 1930 foundation of the Veteran Car Club which was set up for cars made before 1905 – the cars which take part in the annual London-Brighton run. From 1943, they also included the 1905-1919 cars that the English call Edwardians. The Vintage Sports-Car Club was formed in 1936 for Vintage (pre-1931) cars because they believed that the advent of mass production marked the end of proper motor cars; they later retracted to some extent by accepting certain cars of the 'thirties as Post-Vintage Thoroughbreds and even later extended their interests to post-war front-engined *Grand Prix* cars, termed Historic Racing Cars. Post-war divisions and names have rather run out of imagination; it is only the racing fraternity that needs tight year definitions to recapture previous eras, leaving the rest to make do with marques and models, decades or the overall age of the car. So a convenient, all-embracing term like Classic was very necessary to provide an umbrella for all the post-war cars that generate a following.

While Classic *is* used to apply to pre-war cars, most people consider that the classic era covers

*With little change from the pre-war design, the MG TC was the first sports-car on the post-war market.*

post-war cars, which can now be up to 50 years old. The classics in this book are all post-war cars, although some of their stories may start before the war. Within the 44 double-page spreads 132 classics are featured in some detail, ranging from the cheapest with which you can join some form of classic car club through to the most expensive classics of tomorrow. There are a number of American models, too, which are just as likely to have supporting clubs in any country as will the British and Continental equivalents.

It is the classic car clubs that are the backbone of the classic movement. Pre-war cars are covered by marque and general interest clubs, but most post-war cars will be covered by the marque or even model club. Almost any obsolete car will have a car club somewhere, and this should be your first port of call if you are thinking of buying a classic; there may even be one for sale from a club member in the newsletter – it is best to buy a known quantity. If not, there will be a club official who will be happy to guide you to the right model and tell you what to look for. Where to find the club?

There are a number of classic magazines whose pages or enquiry desk will give you club secretary addresses. The magazines will also tell you when the major classic events are taking place; the big classic car shows and concours couldn't function without the help of the clubs, many of whom will have stands or gathering points at these events. If you haven't been a part of the classic scene before, don't rush into a purchase; talk to as

many other owners as possible beforehand. Unless you want to do a lot of restoration work yourself at zero cost per hour, you are always best to buy a restored example; the high cost of a professional restoration plus the cost of the purchase will always leave you on the downside if you need to sell quickly. If you want to join in the fun, but don't know what to buy choose a car with good spares availability; many car clubs make their own spares and there are also many specialists in the various models. If you buy an ex-British Leyland model, there is the whole backing of British Motor Heritage with archives and spares to draw upon.

What else do the clubs offer? All have newsletters of varying standards and all arrange gatherings whether these are competitive or not. They may be concours or driving tests, swap-meets or sprints. Whatever it is, you will soon find that a car club will add another dimension to your social life. You may think that insurance will be an expensive deterrent but it isn't. Most clubs have access to a specialist insurance broker who knows the classic car scene well and will offer low premiums for low annual mileages – 3-5,000 miles a year is a typical level – and they know that the classic owner is going to drive in a way that will preserve his investment.

So take a look through these pages and hopefully you will gain some inspiration either to join the classic movement or to change marques within it. Happy dreaming and then, happy classic motoring.

*Once the Chevrolet Corvette took on V-8 power, it became America's own sporting car; this 1959 model is from the second generation.*

*'The classics in this book are all post-war cars, although some of their stories may start before the war.'*

7

# AC ACE, ACECA, COBRA 289

*'Ace-Bristol was to prove very effective on the race tracks at the end of the 'fifties.'*

From their home in Thames Ditton, Surrey, AC were never a large manufacturer. Starting in 1903 with the Autocarrier, they always produced cars which were well engineered to the standards of the times, but not very exciting. After the last war they continued to produce the elegant tourers and sports cars which had served them well during the 'thirties, but these were inevitably becoming old-fashioned. They needed a new range.

Meanwhile an enthusiastic Cambridge engineer, John Tojeiro, had been building a few specials for club racing. British sports cars had fairly basic chassis designs in 1950, so Tojeiro decided to produce something more sophisticated. The frame was modelled on the successful pre-war BMW 328 with twin large diameter tubes to which was attached an independent front suspension system using a transverse leaf spring with lower wishbones; he used the same system at the rear. The aluminium body was wrapped around small diameter tubes and looked very similar to the Ferrari that had won the first post-war Le Mans 24-hour race in 1949. One car was built for Cliff Davis with the Bristol 2-litre engine which had been developed from the BMW 328, while a

second had a Lea Francis unit; Davis was particularly successful in the Tojeiro-Bristol.

It was an ideal car for AC to develop as their own road car, initially alongside their saloons which were still using the 2-litre 6-cylinder engine that had originally been designed in 1925 – it was this engine that was installed in the new AC Ace when it was launched in 1953. Old it may have been, but it was still good for 85 bhp when equipped with three SU carburetters; in a car weighing only 15cwt (760 Kg) this gave 100 mph performance and 0-60 mph in 12 seconds.

A year later, AC introduced the Aceca, another pre-war model name. This was the fixed head Grand Tourer version with very elegant lines and used the same 2-litre engine to give comfortable high speed cruising. While the AC-engined cars had reasonable success on the track, the chassis could take more power. So 1956 saw the introduction of the Ace-Bristol with 105 bhp for the Aceca and 120 bhp for the Ace which became a very quick car, capable of 115 mph.

By now AC were beginning to export cars to America, and the Ace-Bristol was to prove very effective on the race tracks at the end of the 'fifties; they had the roadholding but could take even more power. This encouraged Carroll Shelby to install a Ford 260 4.2-litre V-8 into one of the cars in 1961; it worked very well and AC adopted the idea, strengthened the chassis and transmission, widened the bodywork by two inches for bigger tyres, and the AC Cobra was born – now a 150 mph car which could reach 100 mph in 13 seconds. It suited AC well as the Bristol unit was going out of production; lesser Aces would continue to be available with the Ford 2.6-litre six-cylinder engine.

Soon the 4.2-litre was replaced by the 271 bhp 4.7-litre 289, and in 1964, Shelby went several stages on and inserted the 425 bhp 7-litre 427 into a chassis that had been redesigned by Ford using bigger chassis tubes and wishbone/coil spring suspension with ever wider wheels and tyres. While these now very fast cars had some success on American race-tracks, it was the 289 in open and closed forms that gave the

*The post-war Ace was launched in 1953, with the Bristol engine option coming in 1956. This is a 1959 Ace-Bristol.*

| SPECIFICATION | AC ACECA (1954) | ACE-BRISTOL (1958) | AC 289 (1967) |
|---|---|---|---|
| ENGINE | 6-cyl 1991 cc | 6-cyl 1971 cc | V-8 4727 cc |
| HORSEPOWER | 90 bhp @ 4500 rpm | 125 bhp @ 6000 rpm | 271 bhp @ 6000 rpm |
| TRANSMISSION | 4-speed manual | 4-speed manual | 4-speed manual |
| CHASSIS | Twin tube frame with independent suspension all round (*all models*) | | |
| BRAKES | Drum brakes | Disc option/drum | Disc brakes |
| TOP SPEED | 105 mph | 115 mph | 144 mph |
| 0-60 MPH | 13.5 sec | 9.0 sec | 5.2 sec |

Cobras the International GT championship in 1965. The big Cobras were not sold in Europe, but AC used the revised (Mk.III) chassis as the AC 289, 4 inches wider than the original leaf-sprung 289 and arguably the nicest of all the V-8 powered ACs in looks and road manners.

While production of the Mk.III ceased in 1969, AC restoration specialists Autokraft got permission in 1983 to bring out a Mk.IV, a Cobra in all but engine specification – still a Ford V-8, but a modern 5-litre unit. You could still buy a new one over 40 years after the original Ace arrived in 1953 – that's classic for you!

*Left: The fixed head AC Aceca came in 1954, the first one being this prototype.*

*Nicest of all the post-war two-seater ACs was the Mk.III 289, using the new Ford-designed chassis – a 1966 example here.*

# ALFA ROMEO GIULIETTA SPRINT, SPIDER, DUETTO

*'The Sprint engine used twin Weber carburetters and developed a remarkable 80 bhp.'*

A competition heritage stretching back to its 1910 origins has ensured that an Alfa Romeo is always just that much more sporting than its equivalents from other manufacturers. Through the 'twenties and 'thirties, the cars were the ones to beat in single and two-seaters, culminating in the Tipo 158/159 which swept all before it in the post-war years until 1951, when the company withdrew from racing to concentrate on producing road cars in larger volumes than ever before.

Work started on the new small Alfa, the Giulietta, in 1952. It had a pressed steel chassis, independent front suspension and a well-located live rear axle; like its larger predecessors, the 1900s, the new car had a twin overhead camshaft engine, a 4-cylinder 1290 cc unit developing 53 bhp for the saloon car; few other volume production cars had single overhead camshaft engines and no others had two. Unusually, though, the saloon wasn't the first version to be launched.

Alfa Romeo had been state-controlled through IRI (Institute for Industrial Reconstruction) from 1933, and were to remain so until Fiat took them over in 1986. In 1953, IRI sought to raise money for Alfa by a bond issue and offered new Giuliettas as prizes; at this stage the new saloon's platform was developed but the superstructure was still under way. Alfa's way out was to find a specialist coachbuilder to produce a limited run of sporting versions and take some as prizes. Bertone was entrusted with the task of creating and producing the two-door Sprint coupé; demand far exceeded expectation and Bertone had to set up a production facility for it – over 25,000 were produced from 1954-61. The Sprint engine used twin Weber carburetters and developed a remarkable 80 bhp which was enough to give the sleek little car a maximum of 100 mph.

The saloon duly followed in spring 1955 and the Spider came shortly after, a two-seater built by Pininfarina on a shorter wheelbase. Veloce versions of the Sprint and Spider appeared in 1956 with 90 bhp engines and some aluminium panels to reduce the weight for competitions. Two more 'external' variants arrived in 1960 using the Spider

| SPECIFICATIONS | GIULIETTA SPRINT<br>(1954) | GIULIA SPIDER<br>(1962) | DUETTO 1600<br>(1966) |
|---|---|---|---|
| ENGINE | 4-cyl dohc 1290 cc | 4-cyl dohc 1570 cc | 4-cyl dohc 1570 |
| POWER | 80 bhp @ 6300 rpm | 92 bhp @ 6200 rpm | 109 bhp @ 6000 rpm |
| TRANSMISSION | Manual 4-speed | Manual 5-speed | Manual 5-speed |
| CHASSIS | Unitary steel body/chassis (*all models*) | | |
| BRAKES | Drums | Discs all round | Discs all round |
| TOP SPEED | 100 mph | 108 mph | 111 mph |
| 0-60 MPH | 13.2 sec | 12.9 sec | 11.2 sec |

*The Giulietta Spider arrived in 1955 on a shorter wheelbase and was built by Pininfarina. This too had a 1600 cc engine until it was replaced by the Duetto.*

*Opposite: Launched in 1966, the 1600 Spider was later called the Duetto, until it became the 1750 in 1968; the 2000 (1976 here) replaced the 1750 in 1971.*

platform, the Giulietta SZ (Sprint by Zagato) and the Giulietta SS (Sprint Speciale by Bertone) both with 100 bhp and 5 speed gearboxes; produced in low numbers these two were particularly attractive and the SZ was very successful in Italian racing.

Come 1962 and the Giulietta was replaced by the Giulia with a 92 bhp 1570 cc engine on a slightly longer platform. The Sprint, Spider and SS continued as Giulia 1600s   Zagato's 1963 derivative being the competition Giulia TZ (Tubolare Zagato). In the year the Giulia Sprint was replaced by the new Sprint GT, a Bertone design but the first to be built in the new Alfa factory at Arese; Bertone's own Sprint didn;t die, but returned as an economy version with the 1300 engine again for 1964. The Giulia, too, had an economy 1300 added to the range; for a bewildering period, old and new models were being produced at the same time with interchangeable engines. More powerful 112 bhp engines were used for the 1963 Giulia Super and the 1964 Spider Veloce. The Sprint GT spawned the cabriolet GTC in 1965, by which time  the original 1955 Spider shape was looking a little dated.

The answer lay in an elegant prototype that Pininfarina had been developing; with a low nose and a tapering tail, it was lower and wider than the old Spider. However in its introduction in 1966 it

too was called the 1600 Spider; Alfa Romeo launched a competition to decide a name and avoid confusion    Duetto was chosen. But by 1968, the Alfa saloon capacity had increased to 1779 cc and the car become the 1750 Spider Veloce, earing a chopped tail in late 1969. After the change to 2000 cc in 1971, the car was to continue in production until 1993 with only minor revisions, a classic feat second to none.

Originally dsigned as a stop-gap, Bertone's Giulietta Sprint was a remarkable success, and went on to use the 1600 cc engine for 1962/3.

# ALFA ROMEO 2600 SPRINT, MONTREAL, GTV6-2.5

*'The silken six transformed the image and the appeal.'*

Since the Giulietta went into volume production in 1954, Alfa Romeo's four-cylinder cars have overshadowed their bigger brothers that were produced in much smaller quantities. But they were fine cars nevertheless and much rarer. Our chosen three were all styled by Bertone and represent some of his finest work of the 'sixties and 'seventies; the 2600 Sprint dates from 1960, the Montreal from 1967, and the GTV6 from 1974.

After the war, Alfa had continued to produce big six-cylinder cars based on pre-war designs, cars with separate chassis which could be supplied to coachbuilders. They were still thinking big in 1950 when they introduced the 1900, the first unitary-bodied Alfa Romeo; work wasn't to start on the high volume Giulietta until two years later. The 1900 used a twin-cam four-cylinder 1884 cc unit developing 90 bhp. Over the next eight years, the range would include the 4-door saloon and the 2-door Sprint as a coupé or cabriolet with the capacity enlarged to 1975 cc in 1953; fastest was the 1900 Super Sprint with 115 bhp. Some 19,000 were produced of which only 1800 were Sprints. These were the chassis on which the famous Disco Volantes and BAT cars were mounted.

In 1958, the new 2000 range used a new chassis and body styles with the same big four-cylinder engine in its 1975 cc form. Over the next three years the factory produced just 2892 saloons, 3443 Touring Spiders and 700 Bertone Sprints, the latter from 1960. The cars looked good but lacked the expected performance and refinement until the six-cylinder 2600 was inserted in 1962; this engine was modelled on the Giulia unit, still featuring twin camshafts, and produced 130 bhp for the saloon and 145 bhp for the Spider and Sprint. The silken six transformed the image and the appeal; the Sprint became a very attractive 125 mph car. When the Sprint GT 1.6 arrived, it was easy to see where the lines had come from.

The 2600 range continued through to the late 'sixties by which time the Giulia had grown into the 1750 and then the 2000, offering similar performance and accommodation in a more modern chassis; the big cars had become superfluous but the company lacked a flagship. This was to come in the shape of the Montreal, Bertone's contribution to the Canadian Expo 67; with its lines inspired by the mid-engined Lamborghini Miura, the show car was adopted by Alfa to take a de-tuned version of the light-alloy V-8 which had powered the Tipo 33, the company's 1967 return to sports car racing. The Montreal took quite a time to reach production, but was finally ready for 1971 using a 2.6-litre version of the 4-cam, dry sump, fuel-injected engine with 200

*Named after the Expo 67 show for which Bertone produced a concept car, the Montreal went into production in 1971 as Alfa's flagship, using a detuned version of the racing V-8.*

bhp, mated to a ZF gearbox. Its chassis followed familiar Alfa practice with a well-located live rear axle. It was a superb looking 135 mph car, but a short-lived casualty of the fuel crisis.

The next big-engined coupé started its life in 1974 as the Alfetta GT. The Alfetta 1.8 saloon had arrived in 1972 slotting in between the 1600 Giulias and the 2000, which it was eventually to replace. Its particular novelty was a de Dion transaxle system for the rear end. The coupé version followed on a shorter wheelbase. Its clean lines were also to be seen on the Alfasud Sprint from 1976. A year later the Alfetta coupé became the GTV2000 finally replacing the original Giulia-based GT. While the Alfetta continued until 1984, when it was replaced by the 90, a new big-car range was launched in 1979, the Alfa 6. This had an all-new 2.5-litre V-6 with belt-driven single overhead camshafts, a superbly smooth engine that lives on in today's 164. When this was inserted in the coupé in 1980 to create the GTV 6, Alfa once again had a flagship sporting machine. Although its 160 bhp wasn't as powerful as the Montreal's V-8, the neater, lighter GTV 6 was almost as fast – an under-rated car that typifies the Alfa sporting spirit – fine looks and a magnificent engine.

| SPECIFICATIONS | 2600 SPRINT (1962) | MONTREAL (1971) | GTV 6 2.5 (1980) |
|---|---|---|---|
| ENGINE | 6-cyl dohc 2584 cc | V-8 dohc 2593 cc | V-6 sohc 2492 cc |
| POWER | 145 bhp @ 5900 rpm | 200 bhp @ 6500 rpm | 160 bhp @ 5600 rpm |
| TRANSMISSION | Manual 5-speed | Manual 5-speed | Manual 5-speed |
| CHASSIS | Unitary steel construction (all models) | | |
| BRAKES | Disc /drum | Discs all round | Discs all round |
| TOP SPEED | 125 mph | 135 mph | 132 mph |
| 0-60 MPH<br>0-100 MPH | 10.4 sec<br>25.6 sec | 8.1 sec<br>21.7 sec | 8.4 sec<br>22.4 sec |

*Below: Under-rated style; the GTV 6 used the smooth 2.5-litre V-6 in what had started life as the Alfetta Coupé with a 1.8-litre four-cylinder.*

*Above: When the 2-litre 4-cylinder engines were replaced by the new 2.6-litre 'six' in 1962, the big Alfas had the performance to match the image.*

# ASTON MARTIN DB4, DB4GT ZAGATO, DB6

*'A lot of publicity was gained by the claim that this was the first production car to achieve 0-100-0 mph in under 30 seconds.'*

When the 3.7-litre DB4 was announced at the 1958 Motor Show, it was just what the British motoring scene needed, a car to match the Italian Ferraris and the German Mercedes 300SL and hold its place in the top flight of *Gran Turismo* machines. Good though the DB2 had been in its day, it didn't have the outright performance to match even the Jaguar sports cars. But the DB4 had the 140 mph pace and it looked the part; it was styled by the Italian coachbuilder Touring in Milan, and featured Touring's Superleggera principle of using a multiplicity of small tubes to carry the aluminium bodywork. It was also a proper four-seater.

The DB4's chassis was a steel platform made from a number of small pressings welded together in a large jig; given the expected numbers it wasn't viable to make a large single pressing tool. Its suspension system was conventional for the day with a double wishbone system at the front and a well located live rear axle, and disc brakes were used all round. Tadek Marek designed a new engine, an aluminium straight-six with twin overhead camshafts; in its first form it developed a genuine 220 bhp which was enough to give the car a remarkable 0-100 mph time of 20 seconds, ten seconds faster than the 3-litre DB2/4 had managed. A lot of publicity was gained by the claim that this was the first production car to achieve 0-100-0 mph in under 30 seconds.

Much of Aston Martin's credibility had been based on racing success and the 'fifties DB3, DB3S and DBR-1 sports-racing cars had used developments of the DB2 engine. Long distance racing in the early 'sixties was moving towards GT cars, so Aston Martin introduced the DB4GT in 1959 – a DB4 with 5 inches removed from the wheelbase and the engine tuned with triple Weber carburetters to produce a genuine 272 bhp, enough to take the maximum speed up to 152 mph; since it reached 100 mph in 14 seconds, the DB4GT's claim for 0-100-0 mph was under 20 seconds.

Racing thoughts went one stage further in 1960 with the introduction of a new version of the DB4GT using lightweight bodywork from Zagato, also from Milan and thus neighbours of Touring. While the road versions were only a little lighter than the DB4GT, the racing versions could be a useful 150 lbs lighter; the performance was in fact very similar, but the DB4GT Zagato was to prove one of the greatest shapes of all time and with only 19 built, it was also one of the rarest production cars. In 1962/3 Aston Martin also built four very special racing GT cars; Project 212 and 215 were prototypes, but the two Project 214 cars used nominal DB4GT chassis, so the Zagato-bodied cars were really only raced by privateers.

The Project cars were the last Aston Martins to be raced directly by the factory. The DB5 that followed in 1963 was built solely to provide comfortable high speed touring; with its engine size increased to 4-litres, it was faster than the DB4 but couldn't match the lightweight versions. In style it was a DB4 with the cowled head-lights of the DB4GT, but it became the best known Aston shape of all thanks to the James Bond film *Goldfinger*.

Two years on came the DB6 with an extra 4 inches in the wheelbase to make the back seats a little more comfortable; the main recognition point though was the flat vertical tail panel with a slight kick-up on the boot-lid, introduced to improve high-speed stability. Overall the style remained

*Using Italian Touring bodywork, the DB4 was Britain's answer to Ferrari when it arrived in 1958. Convertible versions joined the range in 1961, this being a 1963 model.*

| SPECIFICATION | DB4 (1958) | DB4GT (1959) | DB6 (1965) |
|---|---|---|---|
| ENGINE | 6-cyl 3670 cc | 6-cyl 3670 cc | 6-cyl 3995 cc |
| HORSEPOWER | 220 bhp @ 5500 rpm | 272 bhp @ 6000 rpm | 270 bhp @ 6000 rpm |
| TRANSMISSION | Manual 4-speed | Manual 5-speed | Manual 5-speed |
| CHASSIS | Steel platform chassis with aluminium body panels (*all models*) | | |
| BRAKES | Disc brakes all round (*all models*) | | |
| TOP SPEED | 140 mph | 152 mph | 152 mph |
| 0-60 MPH<br>0-100 MPH | 8.9 sec<br>20.9 sec | 6.4 sec<br>14.2 sec | 6.0 sec<br>14.9 sec |

*Zagato, Milan built just 19 special DB4GTs in the 1962-4 period, although they built a further four replicas in 1989.*

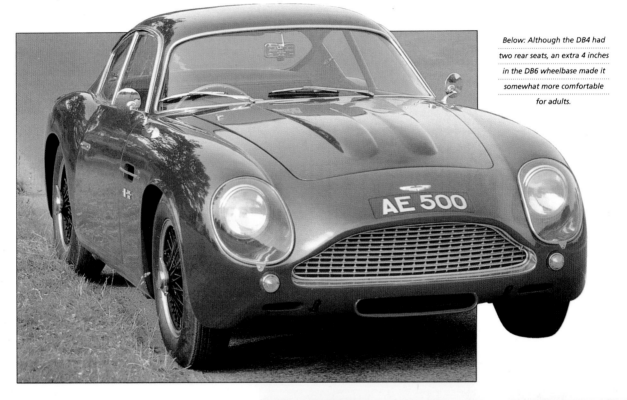

*Below: Although the DB4 had two rear seats, an extra 4 inches in the DB6 wheelbase made it somewhat more comfortable for adults.*

very similar to that of the original DB4, but the Superleggera construction system had been replaced by conventional and heavier steel pressings. The most powerful DB6 had a genuine 270 bhp which gave it a maximum speed of 150 mph and acceleration to match the DB4GT.

By the time the DB6 Mk.II came out in 1969 with wider wheels and optional fuel injection, the new generation DBS had already been in production for two years and the V-8 engine had arrived. Convertible versions of all three models were produced, but the name Volante was only introduced for the DB6 – a DB6 Mk.II Volante is still owned by HRH Prince Charles.

# ASTON MARTIN DBS, VOLANTE, VANTAGE ZAGATO

*'This began to look more like an American muscle car than the best of British.'*

From its concept in the late 'thirties, the *Gran Turismo* had grown from a two-seater with luggage space to the 2+2, for the sporting driver with small children. Many sports car manufacturers have stopped there, unwilling to stretch their cars further into the realms of the

| SPECIFICATION | DBS (1967) | V8 VOLANTE (1988) | VANTAGE ZAGATO (1987) |
|---|---|---|---|
| ENGINE | Straight 6, 3995 cc | Aluminium V-8, 5340 cc with injection or Webers | |
| HORSEPOWER | 270 bhp @ 6000 rpm | 305 bhp @ 5500 rpm | 432 bhp @ 6200 rpm |
| TRANSMISSION | Manual 5-speed ZF with 3-speed automatic optional on non-Vantage | | |
| CHASSIS | Steel platform with aluminium body panels (*all models*) | | |
| BRAKES | Disc brakes all round (*all models*) | | |
| TOP SPEED | 141 mph | 145 mph (auto) | 186 mph |
| 0-60 MPH 0-100 MPH | 7.1 sec 18.0 sec | 7.7 sec 17.3 sec | 4.8 sec 11.3 sec |

*The first DBS models used the old six-cylinder engine before the V-8 came in 1969; this is one of the prototypes which came in between.*

saloon. But Aston Martin moved on to ensure that the keen owner didn't have to sell the car when his children got too big, and he could reasonably consider using it as company transport. The DB4 and DB5 could just carry four adults, the DB6 made the back seat comfortable for longer

journeys, but the DBS was conceived to carry four adults and luggage for as far as they wanted, in as much comfort as could be expected back in 1967.

Although three of the major Italian design houses – Bertone, Touring and Zagato – had been associated with various DB4 models, the DBS was the work of Aston's own young designer William Towns. It followed the classic fast-back shape, but brought in elements of the British razor-edge where top joined side; in its early days with the edges still sharp it had a graceful elegance that it was to lose as humps and protrusions were added during the 20 years that it was to stay in production.

The problem with adding refinement and space is that weight and size increase, so you need a bigger engine to run at the same speed, let alone keep ahead of the field. The new V-8 engine, designed for the DBS, still wasn't ready when the rest of the car was poised to start production, so the top DB6 engine was inserted, the 4-litre straight-6 developing 280 bhp; while this propelled the DB6 at 150 mph, the heavier wider DBS would only manage 140 mph and was left behind in the dash from the lights. But that really didn't matter too much; it was a far more refined car. When the 5.3-litre V-8 arrived two years later it used Bosch fuel injection to deliver 315 bhp and a lot more torque; straight away it was a 160 mph motorcar – refinement now with performance.

Over the years, emission laws have made it harder to produce the power, so the standard V-8 was producing just 305 bhp twenty years later, once more with fuel injection, but very much cleaner. Meanwhile a Vantage high performance version had arrived in 1977 with 375 bhp; with wider wheel arch flares, a kick-up tail spoiler and a front air-dam, this began to look more like an American muscle car than the best of British – ten years of panel beating had worn the sharp edges of the formers too, so the lines were no longer so well defined.

The convertible Volante followed a year later in response to American demand and remained a very popular model until it was replaced in 1989; it is still very much in classic demand, as many prefer its lines to those of the current Virage. For most of its life it was powered by the standard V-8, but towards the end there were Vantage Volantes with the extra power and the muscular bulges if you wanted them – the Prince of Wales didn't on his latest Volante.

Fast though the Vantage was with a maximum speed around 170 mph, people expected even more from the mid-'eighties supercars although most of those were mid-engined two-seaters. Aston Martin once more tied up with Zagato to produce a limited edition lighter, more aerodynamic body for the Vantage for which Aston would produce a special 430 bhp version of the faithful 5.3-litre V-8; launched as a concept in 1986, the Vantage Zagato started production in 1987. With the full 430 bhp and gearing to match, the car tested recorded 299 km/h (186 mph) – just short of the target 300 km/h; most, though, were made with a smaller quieter exhaust system and gearing more suited to traffic. Just 51 were produced before a more

exclusive convertible version arrived, the Volante Zagato; only 36 of these were built and used the 305 bhp fuel injection engine, so their bonnets lacked the Vantage hump.

The DBS was a very elegant car in its own right, but it spawned some fascinating derivatives too.

*The elegant Volante remained one of the most popular V-8 models from its 1978 inception through to 1989; a 1980 model is shown.*

*To put the name up amongst the 300 km/h supercars, Aston Martin returned to Zagato to clothe a 430 bhp version of the Vantage. This 1987 car was the 22nd out of a 51-car run.*

# AUSTIN-HEALEY 100/4, SPRITE, 3000

*'It was certainly a genuine 100 mph car which was an instant success.'*

Following the war, British motor industry policy was to export as much as possible in the quest for harder currencies, America being the obvious target. But the product had to be right too. Lord Nuffield's MG had already established its name. Leonard Lord's 1948 Austin Atlantic – styled specifically for the American market – failed and had gone by 1952. Lord needed a proper British sports car, so he approached two established members of the sports car set in early 1952, Jensen and Frazer Nash to propose a new design using Austin components. He knew that Donald Healey was working on a similar car as he had already agreed to provide A90 engines and gearboxes. All three were planning to exhibit their 'Austins' at the 1952 Motor Show.

Frazer Nash simply inserted an A90 engine, gearbox and back axle into an existing model which could never have been volume produced. Jensen produced a nice looking coupé but didn't make the show. The Healey 100 arrived late but made an instant impact on visitors including Leonard Lord and Lord Nuffield – Austin having merged with Morris earlier that year to make BMC. That night, Healey and Lord agreed terms and the next day the car was rebadged as an Austin-Healey.

The new 100 used a simple platform chassis which was mated to the Gerry Coaker designed body by Jensen, who gained the contract to assemble body-chassis units for all the big Austin-Healeys, bar a handful, for Austin to assemble at Longbridge, before this was transferred to Abingdon in late 1957. The A90 engine was a simple low-revving four-cylinder which developed 90 bhp in Healey tune; the initial series used the A90 gearbox without first gear, but coupled the upper two ratios to a Laycock overdrive to give a choice of five gears. Maximum speeds obtained by the magazines varied from 101 to 108 mph depending mostly on whether the ingenious screen was folded flat or not, but it was certainly a genuine 100 mph car which was an instant success. A second series in 1955 brought in a 4-speed gearbox from the 6-cylinder A90, still with an overdrive which was to remain a big Healey feature.

*Based on Austin A90 components, the Healey 100 was a simple but very effective design which marked the transition from cycle-winged MGs to modern style, here a 1955 example.*

Although the 100M engine modifications could take the output to 110 bhp, and the competition S would produce 132 bhp, a new 102 bhp 2639 cc Austin 6-cylinder unit was inserted in 1956 to make the 100/6 a smoother and slightly faster car. For 1959 this was enlarged to 2912 cc and the legendary Healey 3000 was born. Over the next nine years the power was gradually increased from the initial 124 bhp to 150 bhp for the 3000 Mk.III, by which time the car had wind-up windows and a wooden dash to make it a very civilised road sports car, still with the good looks of the original 100, albeit in a chassis that had been lengthened to take the six.

Throughout its life the big Healey was an effective competition car, particularly in rallying, even when long-distance road events changed to forestry stages where the Healey's limited ground clearance could be a problem – they used side exhausts. It finally ceased production in 1968 when American safety laws became too stringent; despite the fact that over 80 per cent of the 73,000 big Healeys went to America, it was judged too costly to modify the design.

| SPECIFICATIONS | 100/4 (1952) | 3000 Mk.III (1964) | Sprite (1958) |
|---|---|---|---|
| ENGINE | 4-cyl , 2660 cc | 6-cyl 2912 cc | 4-cyl 948 cc |
| POWER | 90 bhp @ 4000 rpm | 150 bhp @ 5250 rpm | 43 bhp @ 5200 rpm |
| TRANSMISSION | Manual 3-speed & o/d | Manual 4-speed & o/d | Manual 4-speed |
| CHASSIS | Unitary steel chassis (all models) | | |
| BRAKES | Drums | Disc/drum | Drums |
| TOP SPEED | 103 mph | 122 mph | 83 mph |
| 0-60 MPH 0-100 MPH | 11.7 sec | 9.8 sec 23.7 sec | 20.5 sec — |

At the time that the big Healey was about to become a six-cylinder, Donald Healey was working on a little sister using the A-series power train, thus giving BMC a complete sports car range; the MGA used the B-series and the big Healey the C-series. The new Austin-Healey Sprite, the original frog-eye, came out in 1958 with a little 948 cc engine producing 43 bhp; while this was less than even an MG TC, its light weight and full-width bodywork allowed it a maximum speed of over 80 mph and reasonable acceleration – it wasn't fast but it was a very good, cheap sports car. Unfortunately it lost its cheeky looks when the Mk.II came out with a parallel MG Midget in 1961. Over the ensuing years, the engine was gradually uprated to 1275 cc and the last Sprite and the last Austin-Healey were built in 1971.

*Above: The frog-eye Sprite arrived in 1958 using the BMC A-series engine in a new unitary chassis, to give cheap 80 mph performance for the young enthusiast.*

*Left: The big Healey gained a 2.6-litre six-cylinder engine in 1956; this became the 3000 in 1959. This Mk.II version has the nominal extra rear seats.*

# BENTLEY CONTINENTAL

Only a handful of British cars have won the great 24-hour race at Le Mans, and Bentley won it five times in the period 1924-30. Then came the Depression and Bentley was taken over by Rolls-Royce in 1931, but the Le Mans reputation has been preserved; the Bentley has always been considered as the sporting Rolls even though the basic engines have been shared. Through the 'thirties, the Bentley was 'The Silent Sports Car', the cars very different in outward appearance and their engines more powerful. In the post-war period, most Rolls models have had a matching Bentley with just a radiator change, but there have been a number of more sporting

*The R-type Continental was one of the most desirable cars of all in the early 'fifties, combining genuine high performance with Bentley comforts.*

Bentleys with no Rolls equivalent; some have simply had more sporting bodywork, others have had more power. Over the period from 1952, the Continentals have mostly offered both; more performance and their own distinctive lines.

First of these were the 1952 R-type Continentals, based on the Bentley R-type and Rolls Silver Dawn. Both were available as chassis only for the coachbuilders and a handful were bodied by other specialists, but the true Continental was only bodied by H.J. Mulliner. Quite unlike any previous standard model, it featured a streamlined body with a long sloping tail, flanked by rear wings finishing in razor-edged fins; powered by an improved version of the standard 4566 cc six-cylinder, the prototype lapped the banked Montlhery circuit at 118 mph at a time when the standard saloon could only just achieve 100 mph; the Continental had a higher back axle ratio as well as closer ratios in the manual gearbox – it would do nearly 80 mph in second gear!

That such a normally conservative company could produce a car designed unashamedly for high speed was largely due to the Paris distributor, Walter Sleator, and Bentley's chief engineer, Ivan

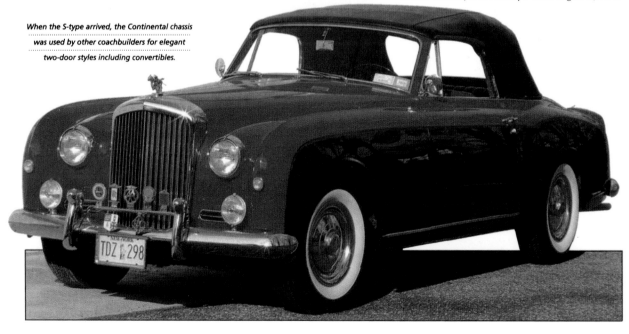

*When the S-type arrived, the Continental chassis was used by other coachbuilders for elegant two-door styles including convertibles.*

Evernden. They were responsible for the creation of La Streamline, a 1938 4.25-litre with a striking fastback body by Van Vooren, commissioned for Andre Embiricos. The factory, too, had van Vooren create the Corniche in 1939; it too featured a non-Bentley radiator, but its fastback was interrupted by a small boot bulge. The next stage in the saga moves to the 1948 Paris Motor Show for which Sleator commissioned Pinin Farina (still a separated name then) to produce a new 2-door fastback saloon. Its profile followed that of the epochal Cisitalia GT, while the frontal aspect featured a Bentley grille of altered proportions; the grille was changed for 1950. Bentley's John Blatchley then made subtle alterations to what had been termed Corniche II, insetting the headlights from the wings, installing a proper full Bentley radiator and breaking up the flanks with a pronounced rear wing line. The resultant Continental was launched in 1952 as the world's fastest four-seater.

When Bentley introduced the S-type with a 4.9-litre engine, the Mulliner Continental continued alongside Park Ward's saloon and convertible versions. The fastback shape ceased in 1959 after a total of 411 had been built, due to the introduction of the S2 with the new V-8 engine which brought the saloon performance up to Continental levels. The Continental name was subsequently used to separate equivalent Rolls and Bentley models, but 1985 saw the first stage of bringing back a separate Continental model. At the Geneva Show, the company displayed a prototype two-door fast-back, the work of John Heffernan and Ken Greenley; called the Bentley 90, it was the forerunner of the new Continental R launched in 1991 using the 6.75-litre Turbo R model as a base.

Rolls had introduced the Mulsanne name (after the Le Mans straight) in 1980 to separate the Bentley from the identical Rolls Silver Spirit, but the introduction of the 320 bhp Mulsanne Turbo in 1982 was a positive move to establish separate marque identities (Rolls have never published power figures). This became the Turbo R in 1985. The big turbo engine received a 40 bhp increase in 1993, and in 1994 a limited S version was introduced with over 400 bhp. These engines are used in the Continental R and S to create the first Bentleys to exceed 150 mph, although the S was discontinued at the beginning of 1995. However the Bentley Continental is back with a classic vengeance.

*'It would do nearly 80 mph in second gear!'*

| SPECIFICATIONS | R-TYPE (1952) | S-TYPE (1956) | R (1991) |
|---|---|---|---|
| ENGINE | 6-cyl 4566 cc | 6-cyl 4887 cc | Turbo V-8 6750 cc |
| POWER | Not quoted | Not quoted | c.360 bhp @ 4200 rpm |
| TRANSMISSION | Manual 4-speed | Manual 4-speed | Auto 4-speed |
| CHASSIS | Separate steel chassis with steel body | | Unitary steel |
| BRAKES | Drums | Drums | Discs with ABS |
| TOP SPEED | 117 mph | 120 mph | 152 mph |
| 0-60 MPH | 13.5 sec | 12.9 sec | 6.2 sec |

# BMW 507, 3.0CSL, 635CSi

*'Only just over 1000 CSLs were built and it has remained a desirable classic.'*

Bayerische Motoren Werke has its roots in the building of World War I aero engines; the blue and white roundel comes from the image of a spinning propeller. The production of engines for planes, trucks and cars, was to continue through the 'twenties, with the company starting its famed motor cycle range in 1923 with the flat-twin shaft drive R32; the configuration has remained unchanged. But it wasn't until they took over the Eisenach Dixi company in 1928 that the company finally became motor manufacturers.

| SPECIFICATION | 507 (1956) | 3.0CSL (1971) | 635CSi (1978) |
|---|---|---|---|
| ENGINE | Aluminium V-8, 3168 cc | Straight-6, 3003 cc | Straight-6, 3453 cc |
| POWER | 155 bhp @ 5000 rpm | 200 bhp @ 5500 rpm | 218 bhp @ 5200 rpm |
| TRANSMISSION | Manual 4-speed | Manual 5-speed | Manual 5-speed |
| CHASSIS | Steel frame | Unitary steel/ali panels | Unitary steel |
| BRAKES | Drums | Discs all round | Discs all round |
| TOP SPEED | 125 mph | 134 mph | 140 mph |
| 0-60 MPH 0-100 MPH | 8.8 sec 22.6 sec | 7.8 sec 20.2 sec | 8.4 sec 19.8 sec |

*BMW production started slowly after the war with large saloons. The first sports car came in 1956, the 507, which went as well as it looked with a 155 bhp 3.2-litre V-8.*

While there had been Dixis large and small, it was the production of the Austin 7 under licence that formed the basis of the BMW cars that were to follow. Early BMWs were small cars recognisably based on the Austin 7, but 1932 saw the arrival of the 3/20 as the first true BMW. A year later the 303 was launched with a little 1173 cc six-cylinder overhead valve engine in a twin-tube chassis with independent front suspension, first of the line that was to yield such sporting legends as the 2-litre 328 and the coupé 327/80 which formed the basis of the first post-war Bristol.

After the war, BMW production could only start slowly with revised, and bigger versions, of the pre-war cars, the 501 appearing in 1951. The 502 followed with an all-aluminium 2.6-litre V-8; this engine, enlarged to 3.2-litres, was used in the first post-war coupé and its convertible equivalent the 1956 503, as well as the short-wheelbase 507 two-seater sports car; with 150 bhp this was a 125 mph sporting machine of very elegant style. But all the 50 series cars were produced in small numbers, 6000 502s over seven years and only 253 of the 507 in four years; BMW's volume manufacture was concentrated on the Isetta, using a motorcycle engine in what was initially just a town car before it grew to the 700 range.

A major shake-up brought an all-new range out in 1961, the four-door 1500 with a style and an

*The 3.0CSL was very similar to the CSi but formed the basis of the racing version; with all its extras, it could look like this 'Batmobile'.*

engine design that has continued recognisably through to the present day. When the four-cylinder grew to six with the 1968 2500 range, BMW moved back into the luxury class and brought out a coupé version once more, the 2800CS; that style was to stay through to 1975 by which time it had become the 3.0CSi. This was the basis for BMW's touring car racing entry, the CSL which used aluminium panels for its bonnet, boot and doors; a small bore increase in 1972 gave it just over 3-litres to change its racing class and a longer stroke in 1973 gave it 3.2-litres and 206 bhp. Only just over 1000 CSLs were built and it has remained a desirable classic, separated visually from its more numerous cousins by discreet coach-lines.

Meanwhile BMW had started to denote the different model ranges with the numerical series which remain to this day; first had been the 1972 5-series. Thus the new coupé replacement became the 6-series in early 1976, starting with the 630 and 633 CSi; while these were quite quick, they were no faster than the old 3.0CS or the four-door 7-series which followed in 1977. It wasn't until the arrival of the 218 bhp 635CSi (6-series, 3.5-litre engine, fuel injection) that the coupé had the performance to match its style, which had been enhanced by the usual sporting appendages – a front air-dam, a boot lid spoiler and coach-lines.

By the time BMW's motorsport division had produced the M635CSi in 1983 with a new 4-valve twin-overhead camshaft engine with 286 bhp, it had become a very fast car capable of over 150 mph; brakes and suspension had been suitably uprated. While most BMW coupés had been saloons with mildly altered two-door bodywork, 6-series was a separate model in its own right – a prelude to its 8-series replacement.

*With the 6-series, BMW coupés returned to their own individual styles. With the Motorsport divisions' M-series came further body changes and 286 bhp for the M6.*

# CHEVROLET BEL AIR, CORVAIR, CAMARO

*'Its long bonnet low roof, short tail ponycar hallmarks would match many GTs.'*

Chevrolet wasn't the first to join General Motors; William Durant created that around Buick in 1908, and was in trouble by 1911. He left to form Chevrolet; five years later he exercised a reverse take-over and once more headed the giant. Chevrolet eventually became the model for the multitude. While the corporation developed economies of scale in the supplies of parts, each division retained a remarkable degree of autonomy for many years in style and power units.

After the second world war Chevrolet continued to produce their 1942 range, the first all-new model coming in 1949, the Styleline. The Bel Air joined the range as the the two-door hardtop for 1950 during which year Chevrolet offered their first automatic transmission, the Powerglide. Until 1955, the power unit had been a pre-war six-cylinder unit of varying capacities between 3.54 and 3.85-litres; however that year saw the introduction of Ed Cole's small-block V-8, initially a 4.34-litre, which gave a lift to the Corvette as well as the Bel Air's top line models.

This was the era of heavy chrome, tail fins and Chevrolet's new wrap-round screen with its vertical pillars. The 1957 range had everything in abundance and there were 19 models in the range

of which the convertible was top; it had 110 mph performance too with the latest V-8, in fuel-injected 4.6-litre form, producing 283 bhp. The '57 Bel Air convertible was one of the great cars of that fabulous finny era.

Meanwhile Chevrolet had been developing a compact to take on the growing number of smaller imports like the VW Beetle. While Ford produced the conventional Falcon, Chevrolet took the unorthodox route and created the Corvair for 1960 as a grown-up VW with American styling; uncertain of the reaction to a rear-engined car, they styled it deliberately to look a front-engined car, albeit without a radiator grille. The VW design features that influenced the Corvair were the swing-axle rear suspension and an air-cooled engine, a flat-6 2.3-litre with 80 or 95 bhp. It was also Chevrolet's first unitary construction chassis.

The Corvair was really quite a good car; its styling was refreshingly clean after the finny era and the 2-door Monza Coupé was attractive to any eyes. The engine was good, too, but the handling was even-more tail-happy than a Beetle's and safety campaigner, Ralph Nader, effectively killed the car. Even a change in rear suspension to a double wishbone principle failed to convince the

*Heavy chrome bumpers, exaggerated tail fins and a powerful V-8 made the 1957 Bel-Air one of the classic American cars of the late 'fifties.*

*The Corvair had a refreshingly uncluttered style that should have appealed to America as the home-grown answer to the VW Beetle, but safety campaigner Nader killed it.*

American market that the Corvair was a nice car quite capable of taking the 180 bhp of the top 2.7-litre turbocharged version. Production ran through to 1969 but the numbers never justified the bold step of selling a radical design to America.

In the wake of the Compact market for down-sized leviathans came a demand for affordable sports compacts, cars that would satisfy the desire of American youth to drag-race away from the lights, but equally be a stylish second car. The Ford Mustang was first in the frame in 1964. GM had hoped the revised Corvair would find its place in this new Ponycar market, but Nader ensured it didn't. However, Chevrolet had a possible alternative on the back-burner, but Ford had two years of unrivalled sales before the new Camaro arrived. This was an all-new car, not just a rebodied version of the Compact Chevy II. While it was essentially a unitary construction car, it had a separate rubber-mounted front sub-frame for a more comfortable shock-free ride; as with Ford there was a low-cost base model with a 140 bhp 'six' but a host of performance options up to a 325 bhp 6.5-litre V-8; Regular Performance Options – RPOs in Chevrolet language – would include such as RS (Rally Sport handling pack) and SS (Super Sport performance pack) complete with body decals.

The Camaro certainly had style; its long bonnet, low roof, short tail ponycar hallmarks would match many European GTs; like many of those, there was also a version that could be converted for racing, Trans-Am saloon racing with the Z-28 package. To match the regulations, the Z-28 was a 5-litre unit developed from the small-

block 327 cu.in with a forged short-stroke crankshaft with a factory rating of 290 bhp, although a blue-printed 400 bhp was possible; period observers reckon the Z-28 had nearer 350 bhp. It proved to be a race-winner and Z-28 Camaros won their Trans-Am category in 1968 and 1969, after which Z-28 became a model rather than just an RPO.

The Camaro name has lived on through many changes but always a high-style pony car and still with a live rear axle, but even the top 1995 car cannot match the Z-28 for sheer power performance.

*Chevrolet's Camaro pony-car arrived two years after the Mustang, but came with all possible options. This 1967 car has the Z-28 engine with the Rally Sport handling package.*

| SPECIFICATION | BEL AIR (1957) | CORVAIR MONZA (1966) | CAMARO Z-28 (1968) |
|---|---|---|---|
| ENGINE | V-8 4637 cc | Flat-6 2683 cc | V-8 4949 cc |
| POWER | 283 bhp @ 6200 rpm | 140 bhp @ 5200 rpm | 290 bhp @ 5800 rpm |
| TRANSMISSION | Manual 4-speed | Manual 4-speed | Manual 4-speed |
| CHASSIS | Separate steel chassis | Unitary steel | Unitary steel |
| BRAKES | Drums | Drums | Disc/drum |
| TOP SPEED | 112 mph | 106 mph | 133 mph |
| 0-60 MPH | 8.6 sec | 11.4 sec | 7.4 sec |

# CHEVROLET CORVETTE, STING RAY, STINGRAY

*'The Corvette began to develop a muscle-car image that had been lacking.'*

Returning from Europe at the end of the second war, the motor-minded GI brought back an MG; it was the nearest thing for wind-in-the-hair sports car motoring to the Jeep that so many had enjoyed driving on active service. European sports cars were lapped up by post-war America, particularly the offerings from MG and Jaguar.

General Motors were the only ones to pick up the gauntlet with any real determination, starting work on the Corvette in 1951. Styled by the legendary Harley Earl with a chassis drawn up by European suspension expert Maurice Olley it was well received when it was launched in 1953, but its reliance on existing saloon car hardware nearly spelled disaster; a two-speed automatic transmission, and a 3.8-litre six – even when tuned to 150 bhp – did not spell sporting performance when measured against the Jaguar XK120. Sales were slow until 1955 when a manual 3-speed gearbox became available and the first V-8 was installed with 195 bhp; sales improved but it wasn't until the 1956 restyle that the Corvette began to develop a muscle-car image that had been lacking .

Available horsepower increased by leaps and bounds during the six-year production run. The original 265 cu.in (4.3-litre) had 225 bhp in 1956 which gave nearly 120 mph; the capacity grew to 283 cu.in and 283 bhp for the top option in 1957 together with a 4-speed manual transmission. For 1962, the 283 had been enlarged to 327 cu.in (5.3-litres) with up to 360 bhp on tap with fuel injection; the rounded rear end had been given a duck-tail the year before and the Corvette grille 'teeth' replaced by a mesh. Much of the credit for taking the Corvette forward into the high-performance league is due to Zora Arkus-Duntov who had joined GM in 1953, and he continued to be known as the father of the real Corvette.

The first big step in the Corvette's design story came in 1963 with the Sting Ray – a European-type fast-back coupé and an equally attractive convertible. Under the new skin was a redesigned chassis featuring independent rear suspension for the first time, and disc brakes were soon to be an option. The same engines were carried over and the fastest version could almost reach 150 mph, but it was the acceleration figures

*Low nose, coke-bottle sills and a T-bar roof made the 1968 restyle even more European, but emission laws gradually stifled performance during its 15-year model life.*

that were impressive in European terms with 0-60 mph in 6.2 sec and 0-100 mph in 15.6 sec.

From the introduction of the V-8 onwards, Corvettes had been very much a part of the American racing scene, but by 1965 they were being consistently beaten by the 7-litre Shelby Cobras. Even more power was needed. Just as Shelby had taken out Ford's small-block 289 cu.in from the AC and dropped in the big-block 427 cu.in, so Duntov put a Chevrolet big-block engine into the top Corvette; this was a 425 bhp 396 cu.in (6.5-litre) for 1965, enlarged the following year to 427 cu.in. There was always a variety of axle ratios available but Americans preferred the lower ones for acceleration; with such a ratio, the Corvette 427 could reach 100 mph in 11.2 sec, but it was limited to 140 mph – longer ratios would give nearer 160 mph. Classic Corvette enthusiasts go for the last two years of the Sting Ray's production; the emission-conscious 'seventies were to see emasculated outputs severely restricting performance.

The next style in 1968 produced an even more European shape, longer, lower and less aggressive with coke-bottle sills and a neat removable T-bar roof; after its first year it became the Stingray (one word). Initially the same range of engines gave similar performance to that of its predecessors, but from 1972 onwards this declined. Even the big block engine was down to 270 bhp

| SPECIFICATION | CORVETTE (1953) | STING RAY (1967) | STINGRAY (1978) |
|---|---|---|---|
| ENGINE | 6-cyl 3860 cc | V-8 5360 cc | V-8 5735 cc |
| POWER | 150 bhp @ 4200 rpm | 360 bhp @ 6000 rpm | 185 @ 4000 rpm |
| TRANSMISSION | Auto 2-speed | Manual 4-speed | Auto 3-speed |
| CHASSIS | Steel with glassfibre body panels (all models) | | |
| BRAKES | Drums all round | Disc brake option | Discs all round |
| TOP SPEED | 105 mph | 147 mph | 125 mph |
| 0-60 MPH 0-100 MPH | 11.0 sec — | 6.2 sec 15.6 sec | 8.7 sec. 25.0 sec |

*This 1954 Corvette is one of the original series with the sluggish six-cylinder engine; the arrival of the V-8 in 1955 set the true Corvette on its muscular way.*

before it was dropped in 1974; by 1978 the 350 cu.in engine (5.7-litres) was only giving 185 bhp. More performance had to come from less weight which was progressively reduced over 1980-82.

The final version of the big Corvettes was the 1982 Collector Edition. The shape had received a soft front end in 1974, losing its chrome bumpers, and a fast-back rear window in 1978; for this edition the large rear window became a hatchback. It was a desirable final fling before the new car arrived in 1983.

*European fast-back styles influenced the 1963 Sting Ray which came in coupé and convertible forms.*

# CHRYSLER 300B, DODGE CHARGER, PLYMOUTH GTX

*'These fantastic looking cars would lap some of the ovals at over 200 mph.'*

The Dodge Charger was Chrysler's other racer to match the Plymouth Belvedere. This 1970 Special Edition has the 440 cu.in wedge-head engine.

This Chrysler trio were all about performance, whether on the street, the drag-strips or the high-speed Ovals. American auto enthusiasm in the 'fifties and 'sixties was very straight-line orientated; roadholding and braking were lesser considerations. Europeans preferred road-racing where sheer power was only part of the equation in making a car quick around a track with corners. Thus, to Europeans, these American classics are rarities; they are each pretty rare in America too. However Jensen, Bristol and Facel-Vega, appreciating the engineering, adopted complete Chrysler engine/transmission units, so the name was associated with high performance in Europe.

Chrysler was a late starter in automobile manufacture. Walter Chrysler had risen through the Buick ranks to become its president in 1920; after a couple of years with Willys he joined Maxwell and the Chrysler marque was created from that in 1924. Four years later he launched the low-cost Plymouth range and took over Dodge (founded in 1914). Chrysler was on his way to make the big two (Ford and General Motors) into the big three; by the time he died in 1940 they had toppled Ford from the second slot.

As with the rest of the American auto-makers, Chrysler's post-war production was pre-war based,

a new range only emerging for 1949; this was over-conservative and a sales slip behind Ford demanded a hefty restyle. This was entrusted to Virgil Exner; having headed Pontiac style pre-war, followed by Studebaker with Raymond Loewy, he joined Chrysler in 1949 but spent his first four years designing idea/dream cars in association with the Italian Ghia company who put them into the metal; Exner's take-over as design chief in 1953 was to draw heavily on the advanced themes established during the Italian association.

A striking addition to the 1955 range was a revised and regrilled 2-door New Yorker called the 300, Chrysler's answer to the Ford Thunderbird; what set it apart was the adoption of Chrysler's V-8, the first Hemi (short for the hemispherical combustion chamber with inclined valves), which had been brought into the range in 1951. With 331 cu.in (5.4-litres) and 300 bhp it was the most powerful engine on the American roads. With this, Chrysler won two stock-car (showroom stock – near standard) championships in 1955, but they only built 1725 of this version. It was the start of the 'win on Sunday, sell on Monday' philosophy in Detroit.

For 1956, the 300B was restyled at the rear with fins reminiscent of the Ghia FliteSweep and the engine uprated still further to 5.8-litres and 355 bhp; 1957's 300C went still further with a 390 bhp 6.4-litre. American manufacturers agreed to stop racing at the end of 1957, and hemi-engines were expensive to build, so 1959 saw a change to wedge-head, still with engines over 6-litres; the 300s were to continue but lacked the charisma of the 300B and 300C.

Racing gradually returned on the manufacturer's agenda and Chrysler built a new race-only 426 hemi (6.98-litres) for the 1964 NASCAR season; after Chrysler products had swept the board, NASCAR rules demanded 500 identical cars. After a year off, Chrysler responded with the Dodge Charger using a 426 street-hemi developing up to 425 bhp; the Plymouth Belvedere followed suit and soon the hemi was available in the Dodge Challenger and Plymouth Barracuda pony-cars. NASCAR racing still occupied the Chrysler mind each year, and 1969 saw the Dodge Daytona Charger complete with droop-snoot nose, retracting headlights and a massive rear wing on tall side-plates. Plymouth's Belvedere had steadily developed through the GTX into the Superbird Road Runner of 1970 to match the Daytona Charger. Chrysler cleaned up in 1970 and these fantastic looking cars would lap some of the ovals at over 200 mph and reach 60 mph in under 5 seconds; although around 1500 were built, NASCAR forced wing-cars to have smaller engines for 1971.

Meanwhile the hemi-option had been somewhat expensive for the non-racer who still wanted to burn up the street tarmac, so the 1966 range also included a conventionally-headed 440 cu.in V-8 (7.2-litre). A high performance Magnum

version (Super Commando for Plymouth) was introduced for 1967 with 375 bhp. A revised Dodge Charger shape came along in 1968, longer and cleaner, and a new 6-pack carburetter was added to the option list in 1969 to give 390 bhp. Chrysler continued their high-power options through 1971, when a new Charger shape came out, but that was the last year of the classic muscle cars.

*The 1955 300 was the first of the American muscle cars with a 300 bhp hemi V-8; this 1956 300B had 355 bhp.*

*Shown below is the 1967 Plymouth Belvedere GTX440.*

| SPECIFICATION | CHRYSLER 300C (1957) | DODGE CHARGER (1967) | PLYMOUTH GTX (1968) |
|---|---|---|---|
| ENGINE | V-8 Hemi, 6426 cc | V-8, 7210 cc | V-8 Hemi, 6974 cc |
| POWER | 390 bhp @ 5200 rpm | 375 bhp @ 4600 rpm | 425 bhp @ 5000 rpm |
| TRANSMISSION | Auto 3-speed | Auto 3-speed | Auto 3-speed |
| CHASSIS | Separate steel | Unitary steel | Unitary steel |
| BRAKES | Drum brakes | Drum brakes | Disc/drum |
| TOP SPEED | 125 mph | 128 mph | 144 mph |
| 0-60 MPH | 8.4 sec | 6.8 sec | 6.3 sec |

# CITROEN LIGHT 15, DS19, SM

*'This was one of motoring's great moments in history, a car so advanced that everything else was hidden in its technical shade.'*

Citroen have long been known for producing slightly quirky cars, cars that are out of the ordinary run and frequently herald the way ahead for the motor industry. The company was founded by Andre Citroen in 1913 as gear manufacturers, hence the famous herring-bone motif. Cars came in 1919, with the popular 5CV soon to contribute to a production rate of 250 cars per day by 1924 – a pressed steel saloon version arrived in 1925; Citroen factories were set up in Britain (1926), Germany and Italy.

The famous Traction-Avant arrived in 1934. This set Citroen on the front-wheel-drive path; the compact power train system had obvious advantages which would be proved with time, but the distinguishing feature then was the attractively low lines that could be achieved without a prop-shaft – the gear lever came through the dashboard. With independent torsion bar suspension at the front and a light beam axle at the rear, it was also advanced in comfort. Its construction, too, was *avant-garde* with a pressed steel unitary frame while the engine was an overhead valve unit with pressed in wet liners – both features well in advance of others. Initially the engine range covered 1303 cc – the French 7 was the English Super Modern 12 – and 1529 cc 7S; for 1935 both were given a longer stroke, so the 7 grew to 1628 cc which was still

called a 12HP as the English system calculated tax horsepower on the engine bore regardless of stroke, the French using a different system. The 7S with 1911 cc became the *Onze Legere*, the English Light 15, and the longer *Onze Normale* became the Big 15.

For 1939, a six-cylinder 2.9-litre (same bore and stroke as the 1911cc four) was added – 15CV for the French and 22.6HP for the English who just called it the Six.

The Light 15 and Six continued in production after the war until 1955, although a French *Onze Legere* was still available until 1957. It was a remarkable production span for a car that was still very modern in design. For 1954, the Six had been given oleo-pneumatic independent rear suspension as a prelude to the launch of the DS19 the following year.

This was one of motoring's great moments in history, a car so advanced that everything else was hidden in its technical shade, even the 'Mark I' Jaguar of the same year. To start with, it was aerodynamically styled by the same Bertoni who had designed the Light 15 shape; it had no obvious grille as the radiator intake was under the bumper line. Its construction extended the unitary principles by having a complete welded-up pressed steel frame with detachable wings and glassfibre

*The Traction Avant was launched in 1934 but it was still a remarkable car in 1953 when this Light 15 was made.*

roof. And the Six's hydraulic suspension system had expanded to control front and rear suspensions, brakes, clutch and provide steering assistance. Even though the chosen engine was based on the old 1911 cc 'four', this had been developed with a new cylinder head with hemi-inclined valves and a twin-choke compound Weber carburetter, so the unit developed the same 75 bhp as the previous Six. Where the Six could reach 83 mph, the new DS19 was 5 mph faster. While it took a little time to learn to drive such an unorthodox car, the rewards came with a very comfortable ride, easy high-speed cruising and spacious, airy seating for five adults.

Over the next 20 years there would be a few changes but nothing fundamental. A cheaper ID19 version had a single-choke carburetter and a normal gearchange; new short-stroke 1985 cc engines came in 1966 with a DS21 having a 2175 cc version. In 1968 the headlights were hidden behind glass as part of an even cleaner front end style, and a DS23 – 2347 cc and 115 bhp – came in 1972; when electronic fuel injection was specified, 130 bhp made the DS23 into a 120 mph car.

Meanwhile Citroen had effectively taken over Maserati in 1969. The Italian company designed a four-cam 2.7-litre V-6 for a new sporting DS, a little shorter, but with recognisable family styling. Given 170 bhp, the SM could achieve 135 mph. While the suspension was firmer and the steering more direct, the basic Citroen hydraulic system was retained; it was a remarkably comfortable high

| SPECIFICATION | LIGHT 15 (1948) | DS19 (1957) | SM (1970) |
|---|---|---|---|
| ENGINE | Four-cyl, 1911 cc | Four-cyl, 1911 cc | Dohc V-6, 2670 cc |
| POWER | 56 bhp @ 4250 rpm | 75 bhp @ 4500 rpm | 170 bhp @ 5500 rpm |
| TRANSMISSION | Manual 3-speed | Semi-auto 4-speed | Manual 5-speed |
| CHASSIS | Unitary steel | Unitary steel | Unitary steel |
| BRAKES | Drums | Disc/drum | Discs all round |
| TOP SPEED | 76 mph | 87 mph | 135 mph |
| 0-60 MPH | 20.6 sec | 23.3 sec | 9.9 sec |

speed tourer which, like the DS, was rewarding once you were accustomed to its intricacies.

Over that 40-year period, Citroen became renowned for advanced technology. Sadly the founder had seen none of its success. He had to sell out to Michelin in 1935 and died from cancer the same year.

*Above: Although the 4-cylinder engine was similar to that of the Light 15, the rest of the DS19 was all-new from its remarkable style to its complex, but effective, hydraulic systems.*

*A product of Citroen's short-lived ownership of Maserati, the SM had a delightful four-cam V-6 power unit that would be shared with the Maserati Merak.*

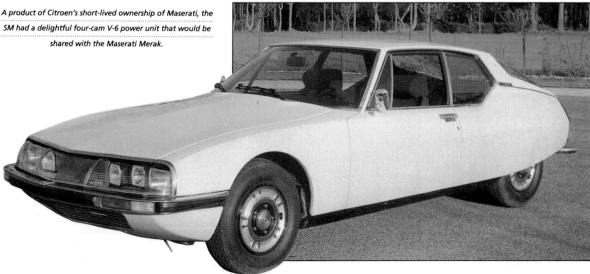

# FIAT DINO 2.4, DINO 246GT, FERRARI 308GTS

*'The Dino 246GT had taken Ferrari into the Porsche market.'*

Although it is always referred to as the Ferrari Dino, the first mid-engined road car to emerge from Maranello was officially just a Dino, bearing the diminutive name of Alfredino, Ferrari's son who died tragically young in 1956. Putting the maker's name first also serves to differentiate this one from the front-engined Fiat Dino which shared the V-6 engine.

Alfredino had been working with Vittorio Jano on a 65-degree V-6 for the 1957 Formula Two racing; that was for 1500 cc engines but Ferrari saw to it that the engine could be increased in capacity to function as a *Grand Prix* engine. The four-cam V-6 had limited F2 success but went on to power Mike Hawthorn to his world championship in 1958. That formula ran out at the end of 1960 when *Grand Prix* rules dictated a change to 1.5-litres; while the original Dino engine was used early on, the team moved on to wide-angle V-6, V-8 and then flat-12.

It was when the 1600 cc formula 2 was planned for 1967 that the Dino engine came back to life. The only problem was that this required a production cylinder block of which 500 had been made. Ferrari persuaded Fiat to produce a sports car using a 2-litre version of that light-alloy engine. Within 20 months Fiat had dived into the parts bin to create a steel frame and partially 'productionised' the V-6 at 1978 cc, while Pininfarina had produced a delightfully aggressive, curvaceous Spider for launch at Turin in late 1966; at the same time, Fiat launched the 124 Spider, also designed by Pininfarina – they had been busy. March 1967 saw longer versions of each as coupés, a Bertone Fiat Dino and Fiat's own style for the 124S Coupé.

Ferrari's Dino came a little later. Its concept was first shown as a Pininfarina styling exercise on a mid-engined 2-litre racing chassis in 1965; Ferrari wanted an entry level model that would take the company into the higher volume 911 market but needed to gauge reaction first. While the concept car had a longitudinal engine and gearbox, the road car used the Fiat engine – with a nominal power increase from 160 bhp to 180 bhp – set transversely with the gearbox contained in the rear of the sump. Shown as a prototype at Turin in late 1967, it finally went into production in late 1968 as the Dino 206, the year in which

*With Pininfarina's Spider and Bertone's 2+2 coupé bodywork, the Fiat Dino 2.4 was one of the best sports cars that Fiat ever made.*

Ferrari's F2 car won a couple of races. Fiat had produced 1163 Spiders and 3670 coupés, and Ferrari had made perhaps 150 Dino 206s when Fiat radically altered their cars into the form they would have liked, without the rush to build 500 units. For 1970, the engine became a quieter 2.4-litre using a cast-iron block, the Fiat box was replaced with one from ZF and independent rear suspension was adopted. Although these were significantly better cars, fewer were produced over the 1970-73 period – 420 Spiders and 2400 coupés.

Ferrari also adopted the 2418 cc engine – 195 bhp against Fiat's 180 bhp – for the Dino 246GT, which became a superb little jewel of a car with near 150 mph performance, remarkable ride and roadholding and wonderful style. Meanwhile the (Ferrari) Dino engine/gearbox package was used to power the highly successful Lancia Stratos rally car – another homologation special of which 500 should have been built during 1973-4; it won the World Rally Championship in 1974-6. That original *Grand Prix* winning V-6 sired quite a family.

The Dino 246GT had taken Ferrari into the Porsche market, but it needed another two seats to match the 911. For the extra weight, a bigger engine was needed. Ferrari chose an aluminium 3-litre V-8, dimensionally two-thirds of a 365 V-12, but with its twin overhead cams driven by toothed belts; this was installed in the first Bertone-designed production Ferrari, the Dino 308 GT4 with 8 inches extra in the wheelbase; although never as highly rated as the two-seaters, the GT4

stayed in production from 1973 until 1980. But to keep up with Porsche's increasing engine sizes, the two-seater 246GT, which had been joined by the Targa-top GTS in 1972, also needed uprating; the 308GTB arrived in 1975 using the same 255 bhp V-8. Early models used glass-fibre bodywork but switched back to steel in 1977, by which time the cars had been officially called Ferraris. Pininfarina's 308GTB has long been rated as one of his best ever styles; it was joined by the removable top 308GTS in 1977. Increasing emission control demands brought a change to fuel injection in 1980, which lost some power, but this was largely recovered by the 1982 adoption of 4-valve heads. It was to be 1985 before the 308 engine was increased to 3.2-litres for the 328 range.

*Never labelled as a Ferrari, the Dino 246GT was the first mid-engined road car to be built at Maranello.*

| SPECIFICATION | DINO 246GT (1971) | FIAT DINO 2.4 (1970) | FERRARI 308GTS (1975) |
|---|---|---|---|
| ENGINE | Dohc V-6, 2418 cc | Dohc V-6, 2418 cc | Dohc V-8, 2927 cc |
| POWER | 195 bhp @ 7600 rpm | 180 bhp @ 6600 rpm | 255 bhp @ 7700 rpm |
| TRANSMISSION | Manual 5-speed | Manual 5-speed | Manual 5-speed |
| CHASSIS | Steel frame and body | Unitary steel | Steel chassis, grp body |
| BRAKES | Discs all round | Discs all round | Discs all round |
| TOP SPEED | 148 mph | 130 mph | 154 mph |
| 0-60 MPH 0-100 MPH | 7.1 sec 17.6 sec | 8.7 sec 19.9 sec | 6.8 sec 16.5 sec |

*First of the 308s was the 1973 GT4, followed by the GTB in 1975 and this Spider GTS in 1977.*

# FERRARI 250GT SWB, 250GT LUSSO, 250GTO

*'The new shape was carefully sculpted at Ferrari to aim for 175 mph.'*

Ferrari is still a great name for stirring the blood of every car enthusiast despite the fact that others have built faster cars or won more races in one or other International category. The 250GT series was the start of serious road-going Ferrari production, and the start of the long-standing relationship with the Pininfarina styling house which has always ensured that Ferraris look as striking as their performance reveals.

Enzo Ferrari loved motor-racing. A successful driver in his own right during the 'twenties, he had then formed Scuderia Ferrari to race Alfa Romeos, before running the factory Alfa Corse team before the war. After that, he decided to build his own cars and the first Ferrari 125 appeared in 1947, using a 1.5-litre V-12 designed by Colombo. Over the next six years, Ferrari produced a wide variety of racing machinery and road cars in very small numbers using different versions of the Colombo engine as well as a bigger V-12 designed by Lampredi. While the variety was to continue throughout the 'fifties, it was in 1954 that the 250GT series began with the Europa, fit for road or track; Pininfarina bodied some 30 of them around Ferrari's simple but effective ladder-frame chassis with the Colombo V-12 now at 3-litres – Ferrari type numbers revealed the size of a single cylinder.

From this point, Ferrari began to build both road cars and raceable cars. To win races at International level you needed a purpose-built car; while a GT car could always be driven on the road, cars designed for the road had become too laden with comforts to be effective track cars. As demand for Ferraris for road use had gradually increased on the back of their racing reputation, Ferrari's 250GT production diverged into the road-going 250GT Coupé bodied to Pininfarina design by Boano and the 250GT Berlinetta dubbed the *Tour de France* after successes in that event.

The racing Berlinettas were given more power from the 3-litre engine – up to 280 bhp – while their bodies were made in aluminium by Scaglietti to Pininfarina's design. Some were more beautiful than others, but all were extremely effective on the track; until the 1959 version, the front end tended to look narrow, while the rear wings ended in light-carrying fins. Come the second 1959 model, the front end had evolved into the aggressive forward leaning stance while the rear wings blended smoothly into the rear panel; this was the stepping point for the 250GT SWB line – arguably one of Pininfarina's top designs for its combination of compact aggression and simple elegance.

All the *Tour de France* models had been built on a 2.6 m wheelbase. The new car, introduced in late 1959, was shorter and lighter on a 2.4 m wheelbase. The simple ladder chassis still carried wishbone independent front suspension and the live axle was supported by leaf springs but well located with four radius arms. The engine remained the magnificent V-12 whose glorious sound had thrilled so many race spectators. This model was soon a success in the GT categories.

However, increasing competition from the likes of Jaguar and Aston Martin forced Ferrari to go a stage further and produce a limited series with lower, lighter and more aerodynamic bodywork; the GT racing rules allowed this, so the 250GTO was introduced in 1962 – O for Omologato showed

*One of Pininfarina's best Ferrari shapes, the 250GT Short Wheel Base was a very successful racer in Grand Touring events as well as an effective road car, for which steel bodies were used instead of aluminium.*

that the motor sport authorities had 'homologated' it, agreeing that it was a production model.

While the 250GT had been capable of speeds around 155 mph, the new shape was carefully sculpted at Ferrari to aim for 175 mph, thanks to a sharper front profile and a better understanding of air flow at the rear, complete with a lip to reduce aerodynamic lift which had made the previous model unstable at high speed. The chassis too was improved with a Watt linkage to hold the rear axle transversely while the engine was further tuned to give 300 bhp, still from the 3-litre V-12. That Ferrari won the International GT category in 1962-4 is adequate testimony to the efficiency of the 250 GT SWB and the 250GTO.

Meanwhile on the road-going scene, the 250GT Coupé with Boano bodywork had been supplemented by a Cabriolet and the California Spyder, the latter really an open version of the competition *Tour de France* cars. The coupé was then replaced by a new model designed and, now, built by Pininfarina from 1958, and still called 250GT; in contrast to the muscular lines of the competition car its slab sides and angular front were elegant but unexciting – people wanted road-versions of the competition car and Ferrari wanted to build them to reach the necessary numbers for GT racing. So this 250GT 2-seater gave way to road-going steel-bodied versions of the competition car in 1960, when it was juggled internally to become the 250GT 2+ 2.

Come the changeover from competition GT to GTO, Ferrari needed another 2-seater road coupé, so Pininfarina created the beautiful 250GT

| SPECIFICATION | 250GT SWB (1959) | 250GTO (1962) | 250GT LUSSO (1964) |
|---|---|---|---|
| ENGINE | V-12 2953 cc | V-12 2953 cc | V-12 2953 cc |
| HORSEPOWER | 260 bhp @ 7000 rpm | 300 bhp @ 7200 rpm | 250 bhp @ 7000 rpm |
| TRANSMISSION | 4-speed manual | 5-speed manual | 4-speed manual |
| CHASSIS | Tubular ladder frame with steel or aluminium body panels (*all models*) | | |
| BRAKES | Disc brakes all round (*all models*) | | |
| TOP SPEED | 155 mph | 165 mph | 150 mph |
| 0-60 MPH | 6.6 sec | 6.0 sec | 6.8 sec |
| 0-100 MPH | 15.2 sec | 14.0 sec | 16.6 sec |

Lusso, *Lusso* meaning Luxury. The same engine was now de-tuned a little to give just 250 bhp.

The main body was in steel, but doors, boot and bonnet were in aluminium. It was the final version of the 250GT series; Ferrari was now an established producer of road cars and the Ferrari-Pininfarina relationship was set to continue to the present day.

*When the 250GT SWB ceased production, Ferrari introduced a new more luxurious two-seater GT, the Lusso meaning luxury; with elements of 250GT and GTO it was extremely elegant.*

*Below: Shaped by the wind tunnel, the 250GTO has become one of the most sought-after Ferraris, and proved a very effective competition car, giving Ferrari success in the GT championship from 1962-3.*

# FERRARI 275GTB, 330GTC, 365GTB4 DAYTONA

*'It had elegance without the poised sprinter look.'*

Fastback styling of the 250GT series was carried through to the 275GTB, but the chassis was all-new with a transaxle and independent rear suspension. This is a 1965 'short-nose' 275GTB.

While the Ferrari 250GT series started as race-cars adapted for the road, the 275 series were the first Ferraris to be designed as road cars; sure the 275 could be raced, but track cars were becoming ever more removed from road cars by this time, and winning GTs had mid-engines.

The 275 was the last of the small-block engines that had originally been seen in the first Ferraris after the war; its V-12 3.3-litre engine was mounted in the front but the gearbox, now with five speeds, was moved to the rear to keep the weight distribution more even. The chassis followed the familiar tubular space-frame principles but independent rear suspension was a welcome change.

The new model was announced at the 1964 Paris Show in two Pininfarina-styled forms, the open 275GTS, which was to be built at Pininfarina's factory, and the coupé 275GTB which was built by Scaglietti, near the Maranello factory. In the GTS, the engine developed 260 bhp at 7000 rpm but the GTB had a choice of two outputs, 250 bhp with three downdraught Weber carburetters, or 280 bhp at 7500 rpm with six Webers. After a year, the body was altered with a

longer nose to reduce front end lift at high speed. The final version came in 1966, the 275GTB/4 with four overhead camshafts, two per bank of six cylinders, and dry sump lubrication; while this was rated at 300 bhp at 8000 rpm, increased torque made it more tractable for road use. During the three year span of the 275GT series, only a little over 1000 were built.

But while the 4-cam version extended the life of the 275, a new 330 range had been presented earlier that year. A new longer block with the traditional V-12 single-cam allowed a capacity increase to 4-litres to give a lazier 300 bhp at 7000 rpm. The chassis design was similar to that of the 275, but a torque tube joined the engine to the rear gear box for smoother, quieter running. Like the 275, it was offered in two body styles, 330GTC and 330GTS; the new shape lost the fastback style and had a lower waistline with more glass area – it had elegance without the poised sprinter look.

The single-cam long-block engine had already been used in Ferrari's sports-racing 330P in 1964; this had been enlarged to a 4.4-litre 365 for the non-factory cars while the works continued to develop the 330 to the point where the 1967 P4 had four cams, three valves, twin plugs, fuel injection and 450 bhp. That 4.4-litre was first used as a production engine in 1967 for the 365GT 2+2, an extremely graceful Pininfarina lengthening of the 330GTC with 25 cm more in the wheelbase but with an overall length increased by 58 cm to provide more luggage space as well as the extra seats; the rear suspension had a self-levelling system to maintain the ride height whatever the loads. It was the following year before the 330GTC and GTS were uprated to 365-series; this was to have a new flagship in the 365GTB4, more commonly called the Daytona as a tribute to the success of the P4 at the 24-hour race and consequent appeal to the American market.

Ferrari needed a classic fast car to replace the 275GTB and it needed to be a four-cam unit to match those of Lamborghini, Aston Martin or Maserati. While the road-engine didn't carry through the P4's 3-valve design, it had new four-cam heads with six downdraught Webers and dry sump lubrication; with 352 bhp at 7500 rpm it was usefully more powerful than the 320 bhp at 6600 rpm achieved by the two-cam cars with lower compression ratios and triple Webers. While the chassis was basically that of the 365GTC/S, the Pininfarina body was quite different, a dramatic reversion to the powerful haunch style of a fastback with a distinctive sharp front end; early cars had the headlights visible behind a perspex band running across the nose, but later ones had this replaced by body-colour metal and the headlamps became swivelling pods. Other variants included a convertible – 100 only – and the 365GTC4, a 2+2 Daytona slightly lengthened

with less horsepower and a revised front end which was available in 1971/2 following the phasing out of the previous 2+2. But the Daytona stayed in production until 1974; over 1300 were built in its six-year life against 350 of the 275GTB4 in just two years.

*With less aggressive styling the 330/365 GTC single-cam cars were softer, more practical and easier to drive than the Daytona; here, a 1967 330GTC.*

*Below: 1973 Ferrari 365GTB4 Daytona.*

| SPECIFICATION | 275GTB4 (1966) | 330GTC (1968) | 365GTB4 (1971) |
|---|---|---|---|
| ENGINE | Ali V-12, 3285 cc | Ali V-12, 3967 cc | Ali V-12, 4390 cc |
| POWER | 300 bhp @ 8000 rpm | 300 bhp @ 7000 rpm | 352 bhp @ 7500 rpm |
| TRANSMISSION | Manual 5-speed transaxle carrying final drive (*all models*) | | |
| CHASSIS | Steel tube frame with steel or aluminium (competition) bodies (*all models*) | | |
| BRAKES | Disc brakes all round (*all models*) | | |
| TOP SPEED | 159 mph | 147 mph | 174 mph |
| 0-60 MPH<br>0-100 MPH | 6.2 sec<br>15.2sec | 6.8 sec<br>15.8 sec | 5.4 sec<br>12.6 sec |

# FERRARI TESTAROSSA,
## 288GTO, F40

*'The shape was really dramatic this time.'*

The big mid-engined Testarossa is a beautiful and very striking car which did all that it set out to do, but during its 1984-1992 lifespan Ferrari brought out two other remarkable but considerably less practical machines – the 288GTO and the F40. As a result, the best of the Boxers never quite had the appreciation it deserved.

The model originally started in production in 1973 as the 365GT4BB, BB denoting Berlinetta Boxer – the flat-12 boxer engine configuration. At the time of its design Ferrari were using a 3-litre flat-12 in GP and Sports Car racing; it gave a usefully low centre of gravity and was very effective. It was a good layout for road cars too, as the width of the engine was not a problem and it allowed a low rear deck for better rearward visibility than many mid-engined cars offered. Making use of existing machinery, Ferrari opted to open out the 60-degree V-12 to 180 degrees which allowed considerable development and component carry-over, although the four camshafts adopted belt drive; at 344 bhp it was a little less powerful than the Daytona due to lower compression ratio and more cramped exhaust system. But instead of putting the gearbox in the conventional racing position behind the final drive, they kept the gearbox mass inside the wheelbase and mounted it within the rear of the sump, causing the engine to sit higher than it might have done.

As ever, the body was styled by Pininfarina but was somewhat understated. Underneath, it used a steel space frame with steel body panels, although the front and rear 'bumper' assemblies were in glass-fibre. Its performance was similar to the Daytona's but the difficulty of rapid take-off with a mid-engined car meant the front-engined one was quicker in the 0-60 mph tests.

While the engine was uprated to 5-litres (BB512) and given a dry sump in 1976, and fuel injection (BB512i) was added in 1981, the first big change came in 1984 with the arrival of the Testarossa, still with 5-litres but now with 4-valve heads and 390 bhp to bring the performance back. The shape was really dramatic this time; the previous front radiator was split into two rear ones fed by giant straked intakes just ahead of the rear wheels, the smaller front intake remaining to cool the brakes. With the side radiators and ever bigger wheels the Testarossa was 6 ins wider than the BB512 and five inches longer. It was a big car compared with the GTO and the F40.

Like its predecessor of 20 years earlier, the GTO was conceived in response to racing rules; Group B required 200 to be built in a year to enable them to take part in GT racing and rallies. Ferrari wanted a weapon to match the Porsche 959 which was the ultimate development of the 911, so they used the 308GTB as a basis and fitted

*Conceived as Ferrari's response to the Group B race/rally Porsche 959, the 288GTO used the 308 as its basis, but used a twin-turbo V-8 set fore-and-aft with a longer, wider composite body.*

twin turbochargers to a 2.85-litre version of the quad-cam V-8 to develop 400 bhp in road form; to allow a conventional gearbox with changeable ratios, the engine was mounted fore-and-aft with the box behind the axle, so the 308 chassis had to be stretched by four inches. While the body was recognisably 308, it was also some 7 inches wider to accommodate bigger wheels and tyres, and made from a mixture of composite materials to keep the weight down. Launched in 1984, it immediately attracted premium prices; unfortunately suitable Group B competitions failed to materialise, but any Limited Edition Ferrari is a classic even without a track record.

Less limited but even faster was the F40 developed to celebrate Ferrari's 40 years of manufacture in 1988. While the chassis used a similar space frame it had carbon fibre bonded to it as lightweight stiffening. The engine, too, was similar but used more turbocharger pressure to

develop 478 bhp from a 2936 cc version of the V-8. Even wider wheels and a latter-day approach to aerodynamics and ground effects saw the latest Pininfarina creation look far more track orientated than did the GTO; the body and interior made liberal use of composites for appearance and weight reduction. While the Testarossa could reach 182 mph and the GTO nearly 190 mph, the F40 all but joined the 200 mph club; they were a fascinating trio from the height of the supercar boom.

*While the preceding BB models were somewhat understated overgrown Dinos, the Testarossa made a bold statement when it arrived in 1984.*

*Under an all-new race-style skin, the F40 chassis was very similar to that of the GTO, but used composite panels to reinforce the steel frame.*

| SPECIFICATION | TESTAROSSA (1985) | 288GT0 (1986) | F40 (1990) |
|---|---|---|---|
| ENGINE | Flat-12, 4942 cc | Turbo V-8, 2885 cc | Turbo V-8, 2936 cc |
| POWER | 390 bhp @ 6300 rpm | 400 bhp @ 7000 rpm | 478 bhp @ 7000 rpm |
| TRANSMISSION | Manual 5-speed | Manual 5-speed | Manual 5-speed |
| CHASSIS | Steel frame and body | Steel frame with composite body work | |
| BRAKES | Disc brakes all round (*all models*) | | |
| TOP SPEED | 182 mph | 189 mph | 198 mph |
| 0-60 MPH<br>0-100 MPH | 5.7 sec<br>11.9 sec | 5.0 sec<br>11.0 sec | 4.1 sec<br>7.6 sec |

# FORD LOTUS CORTINA, CORTINA 1600E, CAPRI 3000GT

When Ford launched the Consul Cortina in September 1962 it was the start of a new design era – a proper four-seater designed down to a weight by current stress techniques. It was a full 100 Kg lighter than the next one up, the Consul Classic introduced in May 1961. Consul was the broad range between the Anglia and the Zephyr/Zodiac and covered three very different models.

This was the period of Ford's Total Performance strategy to capture the youth market. Within a year the Cortina had been joined by a 1500 cc model, the 1500GT and the 'Consul Cortina Sports Special' – the Lotus-Cortina to everyone but the Ford marketing department. In a bid to win saloon car races outright where the Anglias had won classes, Ford commissioned Lotus to make a road-going racer out of the family saloon. Lotus had already developed a twin-cam head for Ford's new five-bearing 1500 cc engine as the

*Although some race teams used other colours, all production Lotus Cortinas were white with green stripes and carried discreet Lotus badges in the revised grille and on rear wings, flared to take wider tyres.*

power unit for the Lotus Elan launched at the 1962 Motor Show. In fact, Ford wanted 1588 cc to make the car better suited to the 1600 cc race category and Lotus subsequently used the same engine for the Elan. Aluminium door skins, boot and bonnet replaced Cortina steel units and wings were slightly flared to take 5.5J rims but the major change was to the rear suspension; the leaf springs were replaced by radius arms while brackets welded to the old forward spring mount dropped down to carry an A-bracket picking up on the axle casing, and coil spring/damper units operated on the radius arms. The springing was much firmer and the car sat two inches lower. Most of the cars were converted from white Cortina 1200 to white/green Lotus Cortinas at the Lotus factory in Cheshunt, but Ford took over once the move to Hethel was imminent.

When the Lotus-Cortina was announced in January 1963 it was an immediate sensation; with 105 bhp it would reach 108 mph and the Elan close-ratio gearbox ensured that it would reach 60 mph in second gear 10.1 seconds after take-off. On the track the car did all that was asked of it,

*The Capri followed the American Ford Mustang in offering a two-door coupé with as many options as possible. This 1600GT was mid-way through a range that ran from 1300 to 3000GT.*

winning races and championships in the UK and Europe, but it wasn't a very reliable road car and certainly had no chance in rallies where Ford stuck to the stronger and less powerful Cortina GT; the rear axle location was the major problem – the stresses were too high to keep the oil in and the linkage was too low for forest rallies. Once the car had been accepted for International competition there was a gradual switch back to standard body panels, but it was to be mid-1965 before the axle went back to leaf springs with additional radius rods – the handling wasn't the same but it stayed together.

When Ford brought in the Mk.II Cortina in mid-1967 there was still a Lotus version uprated to 109 bhp to carry the heavier shell, which retained the same design of lowered suspension as the final Mk.I – regular colours and a discreet Lotus badge made the new one less conspicuous. Part of the Mk.II package was the new cross-flow engine, which gave 88 bhp for the 1600GT, 10 bhp more than the old 1500GT. But the best of the new range was a cross between the two; the 1600E was a 1600GT with the lowered suspension, wide wheels and an executive level of trim – thicker sound deadening, wooden facia and door cappings, better seats and paintwork to match. It was almost a 100 mph car with acceleration not far behind the Cortina Lotus, the new official name, and soon generated quite a following.

At the time of the original Cortina announcement the Classic was joined by the two-door Capri – an attractive coupé that used the 1340 cc, 1500 and 1500GT engines. Such was Cortina success that the Classic/Capri only lasted until 1964, but the Capri name was to be revived in 1969 for a new fast-back coupé evolved along the lines of the American Ford Mustang – long bonnet short tail style with as many options as you can make available. Its running gear followed the usual Ford suspension systems with a choice of half a dozen engines from 1300 cc to the 3-litre V-6, added in 1970; this was uprated in 1972 with an extra 10 bhp and a higher final drive which gave it a 120 mph maximum and Porsche level acceleration.

The Capri – the car you always promised yourself – was a great success running through two face-lifts and numerous refinements until 1987, a final Limited Edition being the Brooklands model using the German 2.8-litre V-6 which had replaced the Essex 3-litre in 1982. While Ford have never made traditional sports cars, they have made some pretty sporting saloons.

*When the Mk.II Cortina arrived in 1967, the 1600E version was a luxury Cortina GT which used Cortina Lotus suspension and wide wheels; it soon became a classic.*

*'When the Lotus-Cortina was announced in January 1963 it was an immediate sensation.'*

| SPECIFICATION | LOTUS-CORTINA (1964) | 1600E (1968) | CAPRI 3000GT (1972) |
|---|---|---|---|
| ENGINE | Dohc four, 1588 cc | Ohv four, 1599 cc | Ohv V-6, 2994 cc |
| POWER | 105 bhp @ 5500 rpm | 88 bhp @ 5400 rpm | 138 bhp @ 5000 rpm |
| TRANSMISSION | Manual 4-speed (all models) | | |
| CHASSIS | Steel with ali panels | Unitary steel body/chassis (both models) | |
| BRAKES | Disc/drum (all models) | | |
| TOP SPEED | 108 mph | 97 mph | 120 mph |
| 0-60 MPH<br>0-100 MPH | 10.1 sec<br>33.5 sec | 11.6 sec<br>— | 8.6 sec<br>26.5 sec |

# FORD THUNDERBIRD, GT40, MERCURY COUGAR

*'The T-bird was still trying to outdrag the Corvette, even if it couldn't out-corner it.'*

Chevrolet beat Ford to the sports car market, so Ford went for the luxury personal car and came up with the Thunderbird – fast in a straight line.

The post-war influx of European sports cars into America caused heartache in the corridors of Detroit power. Ford and Chevrolet responded, but Chevrolet got there first with the Corvette, launched in 1953 despite a 1951 start; it used many standard GM components but it had its own frame and the glass-fibre body was new technology whose short lead-time and low cost tooling enabled Chevrolet to steal a march on Ford. Ford had been looking at a car in the same European sporting mould, but changed tack when the Corvette came out; Ford would create another market and make a two-seater personal car with all 'mod cons' and no compromise to comfort, a two-seater Lincoln.

When the Thunderbird came out in 1955, it had a remarkable elegance and a V-8 engine, two factors that put its sales ahead of the Corvette straight away. The 'vette had started with a sluggish six and was not exactly beautiful; although GM's V-8 came in 1955, and the restyle in 1956, the T-bird got off to a better start. The V-8 was a 292 cu.in. with 198 bhp, enough for 110 mph and a 0-60 mph in under 10 seconds; by 1956 this was up to 312 cu.in and 225 bhp and the spare wheel was mounted on the tail with its own cover. The T-bird was still trying to outdrag the Corvette, even if it couldn't out-corner it, so 1957 saw the addition of a race-level 312 with 285 bhp against

the Corvette's 283 bhp 283 cu.in V-8, but a handful of T-birds were given Paxton superchargers and 340 bhp. In shape, the back end grew some mandatory fins, but that was the last of the classic 2-seater Thunderbirds.

For 1958, Ford added 11 inches to the wheelbase and the car became an open four-seater with a hideous amount of front-end chrome. Despite its looks, it sold well with the increased carrying capacity and engine options that ranged from a 300 bhp 352 cu.in to a big block 430 cu.in with 350 bhp. Fortunately the 1961 restyle restored some elegance, and you could have a two-seater by putting a twin-headrest moulding over the rear seats.

While the Thunderbird has lived on as a luxury sporting machine, Ford needed to get back to the true sports-car image and the Mustang (see page 44) was created for 1964; this had stemmed from Mustang 1, a 1962 show car – a mid-engined two-seater – but became a conventional front-engine rear-drive four-seater. Those that had created the two-seater went on to design the GT40, Ford's racing GT challenge to the Ferraris; while this became a joint design venture with Eric Broadley's similar Lola GT, the concept was evolved in America. Using a built up sheet steel frame with glass-fibre doors, engine cover and front end, it used a variety of race-modified Ford

*From the prototype Mustang 1 came three cars – the Mustang pony-car, the GT40 and the Mercury Cougar. This 1966 GT40 is one of the Mk.I street-racers.*

engines – 4.2 to 4.7 to 7-litre – in a range of shapes. It served its purpose and the 7-litre cars won Le Mans in 1966 (Mk.2) and 1967 (Mk.IV); the GT40 had started as a prototype but, by 1966 was eligible for the 50-off sports car category. When regulations changed for 1968 to limit prototypes to 3-litres, Ford was well poised with the GT40 of which over 100 were to be produced – it won at Le Mans in 1968 and 1969. It was an impressive four years and did much to strengthen Ford's world-wide performance image.

While Mustang 1 can be said to the ancestor of the production Mustang and the GT40, it also added another dimension to the Mercury range with the Cougar. Ford had inserted the Mercury brand between Ford and Lincoln in 1939. In the immediately pre-Mustang period, its Comet range was somewhat bigger than nominal Ford equivalents. The Mustang had the pony-car market to itself for its first two years, but autumn 1966 saw Chevrolet launch the Camaro and Firebird, Chrysler the Barracuda and Ford's Lincoln-Mercury division produced the Mercury Cougar, a name that had actually been applied in-house to the final prototype Mustang II. The Cougar was the luxury sports-model Mustang with an extra three inches in the wheelbase, its own styling – headlights concealed behind a waterfall grille, sequential turn indicators within a rear waterfall – and all the Mustang engine options; it was a good-looking alternative to the mass-appeal

Mustang and came third in the 1967 pony-car sales behind Mustang and Camaro. To launch its performance image Ford campaigned the Cougar in 1967 Trans-Am, but other Mustangs just took the championship. Cougars continue as luxury Mustangs but the first was one of the best.

*Below: The Cougar was a luxury Mustang, with 3 inches added to the wheelbase for more comfort, and its own short tail, long nose styling.*

| SPECIFICATION | FORD T'BIRD (1956) | FORD GT40 MK.III (1967) | MERCURY COUGAR (1967) |
|---|---|---|---|
| ENGINE | Cast-iron V-8, 5115 cc | Cast-iron V-8, 4727 cc | Cast-iron V-8, 6385 cc |
| POWER | 225 bhp @ 4600 rpm | 306 bhp @ 6000 rpm | 320 bhp @ 4800 rpm |
| TRANSMISSION | Auto 3-speed | Manual 5-speed ZF | Auto 3-speed |
| CHASSIS | Steel frame | Steel frame, g/fibre body | Unitary steel |
| BRAKES | Drums | Discs all round | Disc/drum |
| TOP SPEED | 116 mph | 164 mph | 122 mph |
| 0-60 MPH 0-100 MPH | 10.2 sec — | 5.3 sec 11.8 sec | 7.7 sec |

# FORD MUSTANG, SHELBY GT-350, BOSS 351

*'The performance image had to be proved in competition too.'*

Lee Iacocca's quest for the ideal car for American youth started in 1960, the search for a sports car that was more practical and affordable than a Corvette. 'Affordable' meant high numbers and 'practical' required market research, as this was a new arena.

The first prototype was an engineer's ideal, a neat mid-engined equivalent of a Fiat X1/9 albeit some years ahead of even the concept version; called Mustang 1, it was shown in 1962 but, with a space-frame and glass-fibre bodywork, it was impossible to produce in volume. Those engineers went off to design the GT40, leaving others to create Mustang II on the basis of a shortened Ford Falcon – research had shown that the volume American sports car should have four seats.

The Mustang was duly launched in April 1964 in open and fixed hard-top forms, the fastback following a little later. Under $2400 for a base model was remarkable value, but there was nothing special about its simple front-engine rear drive design, it was just the style and the option list that made it unique in that market. Ford were committed to a Total Performance programme and Mustang extras were to reflect this. Initially the engines were from the Falcon range – a 2.8-litre six (170 cu.in.) with 101 bhp and the 4.3-litre (260 cu.in.) with 164 bhp at 4400 rpm; the former could manage just over 90 mph and the latter 105 mph. This lack of sporting potential was speedily rectified in September with the base six now at 200 cu.in and the new V-8 of 289 cu.in (4.7-litre) available in 200, 225 or 271 bhp forms; the last would rev to over 6000 rpm, so the performance was vastly increased to give a maximum of 128 mph and 0-100 mph in 19.7 seconds with the manual 4-speed. Sales exceeded all estimates; 100,000 went in four months and the millionth Mustang came in March 1966, still six months before the first rival appeared in this new pony-car market – the Chevrolet Camaro.

The performance image had to be proved in competition too. Carroll Shelby had played his part with the racing Cobras and was looking for a replacement production racer. When the fastback came out in September 1964, Shelby started work and launched the Shelby-Mustang GT-350 in January 1965 – 350 being an inflated horsepower claim; stiffer springing, wider wheels and tyres, race instruments, bucket seats and some glass-fibre

*Out in 1964, the Mustang was given a minor face-lift in 1967 with a bigger front grille as the most obvious pointer – this is a 1968 convertible.*

panels helped to make it a better track car, while the 289 engine was upped to 306 bhp with a new carburetter and manifold. The Mustang duly won the SCCA Class B against the Corvettes and then went on to win the new Trans-Am championship for saloons in 1966 and 1967.

For 1967 the Mustang had a minor face-lift which made it more comfortable but heavier, so Shelby added the GT-500 to his production, using the 7-litre 428 engine with a lazy 350 bhp. By the end of that year, Shelby had made 4115 GT-350s and 2050 GT-500s; 936 of the 350s used a black and gold colour scheme and were rented out through Hertz as GT-350H. For 1968, emission laws had stopped Shelby making the Cobra and he handed over Shelby Mustang production to Ford, although he still made some convertible versions. In 1968 Ford made 4450 in a variety of forms – GT-350 now with a 302 cu.in.engine, GT-500 with the high performance 427 cu.in engine and GT-500KR (King of the Road) with the 428 engine with 360 bhp. The final year of Shelby production saw another 3150 cars – GT-350s now with the 351 cu.in engine and GT-500s with the Ram Air 428 cu.in engine cut back on non-premium fuel to 335 bhp.

Meanwhile Ford introduced the face-lifted Mustang in 1969 and added the high-performance Mach 1 – after a 1966 show car – and a Grande luxury version; the Mustang was getting soft. And the fastback, now called sportroof, had a race-minded Boss derivative. The Boss series were designed to give Ford the best chance in competition, the Boss 302 with a special stronger engine for Trans-Am and the very limited Boss

429 with 390 bhp to qualify this near race engine for NASCAR. Although they were quick cars they failed to win the 1969 Trans-Am, but went on to win in 1970 by which time a minimum production of 7000 was called for – there are a lot of Boss 302s around. Last of the Boss range was the 1971 Boss 351 which took the Mach 1's 351 cu.in engine out to 335 bhp with high compression and solid valve lifters. It was the last performance Mustang of the muscle-car era.

*The 1971 Boss 351 with 335 bhp is shown here in its sportroof form.*

*Shelby 350GTs were fastback Mustangs built for racing with appropriate chassis mods, some lighter grp panels and the 289 cu.in V-8 uprated to 306 bhp.*

| SPECIFICATION | MUSTANG 289 (1964) | GT-350 (1966) | BOSS 351 (1971) |
|---|---|---|---|
| ENGINE | Iron V-8, 4736 cc | Iron V-8, 4736 cc | Iron V-8 5750cc |
| POWER | 271 bhp @ 6000 rpm | 306 bhp @ 6000 rpm | 335 bhp @ 6000 rpm |
| TRANSMISSION | Manual 4-speed | Manual 4-speed | Manual 4-speed |
| CHASSIS | Unitary steel for hardtop, fastback and convertible models | | |
| BRAKES | Disc/drum option | Disc/drum | Disc/drum |
| TOP SPEED | 128 mph | 135 mph | 135 mph |
| 0-60 MPH | 7.6 sec | 6.2 sec | 6.4 sec |

# JAGUAR XK120, C-TYPE, XK150

From the moment of its launch at the 1948 Earls Court Motor Show, the Jaguar XK120 was destined to become one of the great cars in history. It had a style and a level of performance that transcended anything else that was to appear in those early post-war years. It was just as much at home on road or track with impressive victories in rallies too; while the chassis design was unremarkable, its famous twin-cam six-cylinder engine would go on to power five Le Mans winners and countless road cars before it was finally phased out in 1987.

Before the war, Jaguar was a model name for SS Cars, the company founded by William Lyons on the back of his previous Swallow Coach-building; Armstrong Siddeley used to make a Jaguar aero engine but surrendered the name to

Lyons in 1936. Most famous of these was the SS Jaguar 100 two-seater sports car which generated a strong competition following. The name was changed to Jaguar Cars in 1945 in preparation for the launch of the first real Jaguar.

Much of the ground-work had evolved during the latter part of the war; William Lyons and some of his engineers had been engaged in fire-watching and had used the time to decide what the first true Jaguars would be – a 100 mph saloon and a faster sports car, both to be powered by the same six-cylinder twin overhead camshaft engine which would need to produce around 160 bhp. As it turned out they continued to make revised versions of the pre-war saloons until the 1948 launch of both the Mark V with the old 3.5-litre pushrod engine and the XK120 with the new 3.4-litre engine, both having separate chassis with new torsion bar independent front suspension. The 100 mph saloon would wait until the 1951 Mk.VII. When announced, the XK120s were to be bodied in the traditional low volume way – aluminium on wood – but such was the demand that steel bodies were brought in after the first 240 cars. Over 12,000 would be built in open and fixed head coupé forms with the vast majority going overseas in those export conscious days.

The 120 part of the name signified the speed the car was expected to reach; period road tests all

*When sports car still meant cycle wings and slab tanks, the arrival of the XK120 in 1948 was a major step forward in sporting design.*

*While XK120s did well at the 1950 Le Mans, Jaguar wanted outright victory for 1951; the XK120C won in 1951 and 1953.*

The XK140 was little changed from the earlier car, but the XK150 was a much more substantial and more comfortable car – here is an XK150 3.4 drop-head coupé.

confirmed it. This high performance made it particularly suitable for rallying where the XK120 scored its greatest International successes – Ian Appleyard's four Alpine Cups among the most noteworthy. They were raced, too, with Stirling Moss' 1950 TT win a highlight, and they had also been to the Le Mans 24-hours that year – although they didn't win, one had always run in the top seven before retiring in the 23rd hour and two others finished 12th and 15th. It was enough to convince Lyons that a lighter purpose-built car could win with the same engine, so work started on the XK120C (Competition), always known as the C-type; which explains why there were never A-types and B-types.

The C used a space-frame chassis with an all-enveloping quickly detachable body with considerably improved aerodynamics. Front suspension followed the 120 but the live rear axle was well located with radius arms and an A-bracket

and sprung by torsion bars. With the engine tuned to give 204 bhp, the C-type gained its first Le Mans victory in 1951. C-types were also produced for private racers and would do over 140 mph with 200 bhp. Although rebodied versions failed early in the 1952 Le Mans, lighter versions of the original shape were prepared for 1953 with more power – 220 bhp with triple Webers – and disc brakes; the works cars finished 1st, 2nd and 4th. With two victories in the world's most famous motor race, the Jaguar reputation was well and truly founded.

Thus when the replacement XK140 came out in 1954 it bore a plaque proclaiming the victories. Similar to the XK120, the new car was given a little more interior space by moving the engine forward. With 190 bhp or 210 bhp in special equipment form, the top speed could rise to nearly 130 mph. The model was replaced by the XK150 in 1957 with more comfortable bodywork for the customary fixed head, drop-head and roadster versions, and disc brakes for all; the engine was finally enlarged to 3.8-litres in 1959 with the XK150S 3.8 receiving the 265 bhp which would power the E-type from its 1961 launch. The 'fifties had been an exciting decade for Jaguar.

*'The 120 part of the name signified the speed the car was expected to reach.'*

| SPECIFICATION | XK120 (1949) | XK120C (1952) | XK150S 3.8 (1960) |
|---|---|---|---|
| ENGINE | Straight-6, 3442 cc | Straight-6, 3442 cc | Straight-6, 3781 cc |
| POWER | 160 bhp @ 5000 rpm | 200 bhp @ 5800 rpm | 265 bhp @ 5500 rpm |
| TRANSMISSION | Manual 4-speed (*all models*) | | |
| CHASSIS | Steel frame and body | Tubular frame, ali body | Steel frame and body |
| BRAKES | Drums | Drums | Discs |
| TOP SPEED | 124 mph | 144 mph | 136 mph |
| 0-60 MPH 0-100 MPH | 10.0 sec 27.3 sec | 8.1 sec 20.1 sec | 7.6 sec 19.0 sec |

# JAGUAR XKSS, E-TYPE, XJS

Less well-known than the racing Jaguar D-type, the XKSS was the rare road-going version. Arguably the Jaguar E-type was its direct descendant – a race-bred car – before the XJS took over in 1975.

Having won the renowned Le Mans 24-hour race in 1951 and 1953 with the C-types, Jaguar were keen to continue. Not only did such racing improve the road car breed but success, particularly at Le Mans, brought tremendous publicity benefits. Le Mans was a very fast circuit so a low drag shape was very important; aerodynamicist Malcolm Sayer, who had also styled the

C-type, evolved the D-type with an elliptical cross-section which helped to reduce drag to around half that of the XK120. It made a big difference in Le Mans lap times.

The chassis construction was very different from that of the C-type. Although there was a square tube frame underneath, the centre section was made into a stressed skin monocoque with metal panels riveted to it, aircraft fashion; the frame extended forwards to carry engine, front suspension, radiator and bonnet mounts. To the rear a sub-frame carried bodywork but the suspension trailed from the rear of the monocoque – still a live axle but with twin radius arm plates and an A-bracket. The XK engine, giving around 245 bhp with triple Webers, was converted to dry sump lubrication to keep the frontal area down. The D's first year was not quite a success; one finished second while the Belgian C-type finished 4th. Down the straight, the D had clocked 173 mph, the C 147 mph while the winning Ferrari reached 160 mph. The next three years saw victory for further developments of the Jaguars, although 1956 and 1957 were due to the private Ecurie Ecosse team – the works had stopped after 1956. Although they were built specifically to win

*When the E-type arrived in 1961, it embodied many of the D-type principles, including its monocoque construction and a 3.8-litre XK engine. This is a 1962 3.8-litre roadster.*

*By 1957 demand for the amateur racer's D-type had dwindled, so a number were converted to two-seater road-going XKSS – as this one.*

Le Mans, the D-types won many other races over the period, but by 1957 private entrant demand had slowed; Jaguar decided to produce a road-going version with a soft-top attached to a full width screen, and a nominal silencer for an engine that was identical to the 1954 cars. While over 60 D-types were produced, there were only 16 of these XKSS.

Emphasising that it was the true successor to the D-type rather than an evolution of the XK150, Jaguar's E-type followed the same monocoque construction principles within a Sayer-developed style that was recognisably a stretched D-type – it was six inches longer in the wheelbase and over a foot longer overall which helped to provide luggage space. A major change though was the independent rear suspension which had been tried on the 2nd prototype E2A, which had run at Le Mans in 1960, and was also to be used on the Mk.X announced later in 1961. The XK engine was the same 3.8-litre six that had been developed for the XK150S. On its announcement at Geneva in March 1961, the E-type made just as much impact on the sporting public as the XK120 had done 13 years earlier; roadster and fixed head styles were both capable of around 144 mph, although the press cars were a little faster with the coupé reaching 150 mph for *Autocar*. It was such a well-mannered fast car with a very comfortable ride, that it became everyone's ideal.

Over the next 14 years, the XK would increase to 4.2-litres for the same output but more torque, nine inches would be added for a 2+2 version with a raised roof, and a V-12 would replace the XK engine in 1971 to make up for the power lost in reducing emissions. That V-12 had started life in the mid-engined XJ13 which might have taken Jaguar back to Le Mans in 1966/7; then a 5-litre 4-cam engine, it was considerably refined to become a silky smooth 5.3-litre with just a single cam per bank by the time it was inserted in the Mk.III E-type with 272 bhp.

This engine was the heart of the XJS which followed on, although for this it had fuel injection and 285 bhp. Many decry the XJS as an unworthy replacement for such an icon as the E-type, but demand for overtly sporting cars had diminished considerably after the 1973 fuel crisis, and a more comfortable Grand Tourer was what the market wanted. The central monocoque system had gone and the XJS used the conventional unitary construction retaining the rear suspension subframe; with that effortless V-12 power the XJS was a class leader in quiet 100 mph cruising, a far cry from the wind-swept XK120.

*Jaguar's new V-12 was first used in the E-type from 1971. This engine and the rear suspension design was all that was carried over to the replacement XJS in 1975.*

'*Many decry the XJS as an unworthy replacement for such an icon as the E-type.*'

| SPECIFICATION | XKSS (1957) | E-TYPE 3.8 fhc (1961) | XJS V-12 (1975) |
|---|---|---|---|
| ENGINE | Straight-6, 3442 cc | Straight-6, 3781 cc | V-12, 5344 cc |
| POWER | 250 bhp @ 5750 rpm | 265 bhp @ 5500 rpm | 285 bhp @ 5500 rpm |
| TRANSMISSION | Manual 4-speed | Manual 4-speed | Manual 4-speed |
| CHASSIS | Ali body & chassis | Steel chassis | Unitary steel |
| BRAKES | Discs | Discs | Discs |
| TOP SPEED | 149 mph | 150 mph | 153 mph |
| 0-60 MPH<br>0-100 MPH | 7.3 sec<br>13.6 sec | 6.9 sec<br>16.2 sec | 6.7 sec<br>16.2 sec |

# JAGUAR 2.4, 3.8 MK.II, XJ12C

*'Inside was all the luxury that had become a Jaguar hallmark.'*

*Below: The little Jaguar 2.4 was introduced in 1955; rear wheel spats and narrow grille were distinguishing features up to the time the 3.4 arrived in 1957 with partial spats, as this, to allow wire wheels and wider grille, later used on the 2.4 as well.*

Once Jaguar had launched the Mk.VII in 1950, there was an obvious need for a smaller saloon if Jaguar were to move into any form of volume production. Given the Jaguar reputation it had to be a sports saloon which was a relatively untapped market in 1955. And moving with the times, it was to be Jaguar's first unitary construction car – Mk.VII and XK120 still having separate chassis.

While its engine might have been the four-cylinder twin-cam that had been considered for a low cost XK100, the final choice was a short-stroke version of the familiar six; with twin small downdraught Solex carburetters it produced a conservative 112 bhp from 2483 cc. For the front suspension, a separate sub-frame was used to isolate road-shocks, so the double wishbone system adopted coil springs rather than the torsion bars of the previous models. At the rear, the live axle was located by twin upper radius arms, a semi-trailing Panhard rod while cantilevered leaf springs, set into under-body channels, acted as lower radius arms – in principle similar to the C and D-types.

As with all Jaguars during his rule, the major styling input came from the boss, Sir William Lyons. Where the XK120 maintained the pre-war theme of separately delineated flowing wings, and the Mk.VII followed suit, the 2.4's waistline was a single sweep from the front to the fallaway tail; the whole was a nice balance of flowing curves and practicality, although the rear wheel spats were a little affected. At the front, the XK140 family style was evident in the grille flanked by inset headlights and prominent horn grilles. Inside was all the luxury that had become a Jaguar hallmark with the polished wooden facia and comfortable leather-covered seating for four.

With the optional overdrive ratio, the 2.4 would just reach 100 mph which was good enough for European markets but Americans were critical of the lack of the easy acceleration offered by their customary big V-8s and automatic transmission. This was remedied by the March 1957 arrival of

| SPECIFICATION | 2.4 (1956) | 3.8 MK.II (1963) | XJ12C (1975) |
|---|---|---|---|
| ENGINE | Dohc 6, 2483 cc | Dohc 6, 3781 cc | Ali V-12, 5344 cc |
| POWER | 112 bhp @ 5750 rpm | 220 bhp @ 5500 rpm | 285 bhp @ 5750 rpm |
| TRANSMISSION | Manual 4-speed + o/d | Manual 4-speed + o/d | Auto 3-speed |
| CHASSIS | Unitary steel construction used for all models from 2.4 onwards | | |
| BRAKES | Drums | Discs | Discs |
| TOP SPEED | 101 mph | 125 mph | 147 mph |
| 0-60 MPH 0-100 MPH | 14.4 sec — | 8.5 sec 25.1 sec | 8.3 sec 19.9 sec |

the 3.4-litre version which was easily recognisable by its wider grille, twin exhaust tail pipes and rear wheel spats with a partial cut-out to allow the option of wire wheels. With 210 bhp the 3.4 was a 120 mph car with acceleration to match; the US market was further satisfied by the option of automatic transmission. Disc brakes all round became on option for 2.4 and 3.4 within six months.

Good though the compact Jaguars were, the arrival of the Mk.II in October 1959 brought some welcome changes. The rear track had been uncomfortably narrower than the front so this was increased by 3.25 inches to benefit handling; more glass was added by widening the rear window and giving the side-windows simple chromed frames; the grille had a broad strip in the centre and was flanked by fog-lights rather than horns; and the dashboard was redesigned. It was a much better car; the 2.4 received an increase to 120 bhp, the 3.4 stayed at 210 bhp but the new 3.8 gave 220 bhp and 125 mph. It was the Mk.II 3.8 that gave the compact Jaguar its charisma; not only was it a police favourite in the new motorway era, but it was a very successful saloon car racer.

The shape was to continue for many years including the Daimler variant with the 2.5-litre V-8 which came in 1962. The Mk.IIs blended into a new range of 240 and 340 plus the V-8 250 in 1967 as 'cheaper' Jaguars, following the 1963 introduction of the S-types, 3.4 and 3.8. These were basically modernised Mk.IIs with the Mk.X independent rear suspension which necessitated a stronger rear floor area, and earned a longer luggage boot and more rear headroom in the process. The S-range was extended with the 245 bhp 420 in 1966, its front-end style adjusted to match the 420G which took over from the Mk.X. The somewhat bewildering model range was then all rationalised with the overdue arrival of the XJ6 in 1968.

While the E-type continued to sell, all other Jaguars were XJ6 variants which made for new economies of scale to enable Jaguar to maintain its value for money policy. Launched with 2.8 and 4.2-litre engines, the range was joined by the XJ12 in mid-1972. When the Series 2 cars came in 1973, the range included a new 2-door coupé powered by either the 4.2-litre or the V-12. To classic eyes,

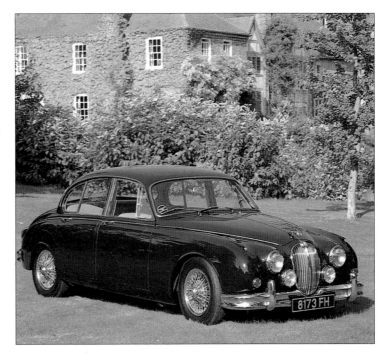

these were the nicest of the range although there were always problems with sealing frameless windows which had delayed their production until 1975; they sadly disappeared in 1977 after 6505 XJ6C and only 1873 XJ12C had been produced – the XJS served a similar function with fewer problems.

*The picture above shows a 1963 Jaguar 3.8 Mk.II.*

*Less than 2000 of these XJ12C were produced.*

# LAMBORGHINI 400GT, ESPADA, URRACO

When Italian tractor magnate, Ferruccio Lamborghini, decided that he would build a GT car that would satisfy his perfectionist tastes, he gathered a core of talented young engineers in 1962 to translate his wishes into design and then production. Giampaolo Dallara, Paolo Stanzani were in at the beginning; New Zealander Bob Wallace joined at the end of 1963 for the development of the first car, by which time the new factory at Sant'Agata Bolognese was nearly complete.

While the trio above all had previous Maserati connections, engine design was entrusted to Giotto Bizzarrini who was to go on to design the Iso Rivoltas and his own Grifo derivative, the Strada 5300. Fresh from Ferrari where he had led the 250GTO project, he followed instructions to produce a more modern engine than Ferrari with more power and came up with a 3.5-litre V-12 with twin overhead camshafts, an extrapolated version of a 1.5-litre racing engine he had designed for Ferrari. While that produced over 350 bhp at 8000 rpm on the test-bed it was then tamed for production durability by Dallara to a still respectable 270 bhp at 6500 rpm. Dallara's chassis was a straightforward tubular frame, but it had independent rear suspension which was then a rarity. Gearbox came from ZF and final drive from Salisbury.

Touring produced the production body which was well received at Geneva in March 1964; despite the short development period, production then started with Touring making the bodywork with the chassis also contracted out – then, as now, the Lamborghini line was a final assembly facility built around a machine shop. After a year of 350GT production, the engine was enlarged to 3.9-litres with 320 bhp for the 400GT, which also used Lamborghini's own gearbox and final drive assembly. Maximum speed went from 148 to 156 mph although the 0-60 mph time was slower than before as the car had put on weight – but 7.0 seconds wasn't slow in those days; it was also a very good GT car.

*The Lamborghini 350GT was the first from Sant'Agata in 1964; the 400GT followed a year later with its 4-litre V-12 producing 320 bhp, as this 1966 example.*

*Below: A 2+2 400GT was offered in 1966, but replaced in 1968 by the Islero 2+2. The 4-seater Espada was launched at the same time and continued for the next 10 years; this is a 1972 Espada.*

For 1966, a 2+2 was added to the range. On the same wheelbase, extra space was found with a 2-in higher roof-line and adjustment to the rear suspension mountings. It sold better than the 2-seaters, so its replacement Islero for 1968 was also a 2+2; slightly taller, but shorter, than the 400GT 2+2, its shape was created jointly by the boss and Marazzi, a group of ex-Touring employees following the collapse of the Milan coachbuilder. It was clean and simple, but was somewhat overshadowed by the striking Bertone-styled four-seater Espada which was launched at the same 1968 Geneva Show.

While the Islero had continued with the old tubular chassis, the Espada followed Miura thinking and used a sheet steel platform. Its body was modelled on Bertone's Marzal concept car; it was longer, lower and wider than the Islero and featured a fast-back with a lift-up window and an auxiliary glass panel in the tail to assist visibility, the car being only 3ft.11in tall. The engine, now with the 350 bhp version brought in for the Islero GTS, was well forward and it was a genuine four-seater; it was a top seller straight away and continued in production until 1978, by which time Lamborghini had changed hands – Ferruccio had sold out to Swiss interests during 1972/3. Meanwhile the Islero was only in production for two years, being replaced by the Bertone-designed Jarama which had adopted the Espada chassis with nearly 7

inches out of the wheelbase – that continued until 1976.

From early on, thought had always been given to a small Lamborghini for the higher volume, lower price Porsche market. It wasn't until the Dino 246 arrived in 1969 that this was put into action – the Urraco would be a mid-engined 2+2 with a new V-8 engine. This was all-aluminium but used single overhead camshafts driven by toothed belt which gave 220 bhp in 2.5-litre form for the P250 – the gearbox was mounted on the end; a sheet steel chassis carried MacPherson strut suspension at each corner and the body was a very neat and attractive Bertone design. First shown in late 1970, it was well liked and production began in 1972; for 1975, the engine was uprated for the P300 with a 250 bhp 3-litre version with four chain-driven cams, an altogether nicer power unit which gave the car a 158 mph maximum speed. But problems in the factory and world economy limited its production to a mere 205 cars by 1979 against 586 of its smaller predecessor. The concept lived on, though, into the Jalpa.

*'The Lamborghini line was a final assembly facility built around a machine shop.'*

*The mid-engined Urraco with a 2.5-litre V-8 began production in 1972 but was replaced by the better 3-litre P300 in 1975. Bertone styled the little 2+2.*

| SPECIFICATION | 400GT (1966) | ESPADA (1972) | URRACO P300 (1975) |
|---|---|---|---|
| ENGINE | Ali V-12, 3929 cc | Ali V-12, 3929 cc | Ali V-8, 2996 cc |
| POWER | 320 bhp @ 6500 rpm | 350 bhp @ 7800 rpm | 250 bhp @ 7500 rpm |
| TRANSMISSION | Manual 5-speed | Manual 5-speed | Manual 5-speed |
| CHASSIS | Tubular frame | Sheet steel | Sheet steel |
| BRAKES | Discs all round | Discs all round | Discs all round |
| TOP SPEED | 156 mph | 153 mph | 158 mph |
| 0-60 MPH 0-100 MPH | 7.0 sec 17.1 sec | 7.8 sec 17.8 sec | 7.5 sec 17.5 sec |

# LAMBORGHINI MIURA, COUNTACH, DIABLO

*'They performed with all the promise of that exciting design; top speed around 170 mph with roadholding at race-track levels.'*

*The Countach finally got into production in 1973 as the LP400; wider tyres introduced for this LP400S in 1978 brought glassfibre eyebrows over the wheel arches.*

Once the first Lamborghini was under way in 1964, the thoughts of its enterprising young engineers turned towards creating a car that could be used for GT racing, which demanded a mid-engined layout. Although Ferruccio Lamborghini would never sanction a racing project, he encouraged the development which was to lead to the first supercar, the Miura P400, with stunning 2-seater bodywork by Bertone's young designer, Marcello Gandini. It was first shown in chassis form at the 1965 Turin Show, and initial thoughts of producing perhaps a handful were overwhelmed by the interest shown.

The difficulty of fitting the long V-12 350 bhp 4-litre into a mid-engined layout was ingeniously solved by setting it transversely, and integrating the gearbox behind it with a complex crankcase casting which could only have been done in Italy. Its chassis followed modern racing style and used a sheet steel centre section with fore and aft extensions to carry the wishbone suspensions and cradle the engine.

The first prototype was shown at the 1966 Geneva Show from which point road development could only just begin; so the first cars didn't leave until early 1967. They performed with all the promise of that exciting design; top speed around 170 mph with roadholding at race-track levels. Two years later it received more power, a stiffened chassis and some suspension changes to cope with wider tyres; the P400S had 370 bhp. The final version, the P400SV, came a year later with even wider tyres requiring some bodywork flaring, and another 15 bhp. In all, 765 were built; production stopped prematurely in 1971 to hand over to the Countach, but that took two more years to develop after its first showing at Geneva that year. But the Miura had put the Lamborghini star in the supercar ascendant.

For the Countach, Dallara produced a space-frame chassis but took a front-engine gearbox unit and turned it round to put the gear-box nearest the driver; this gave a very short and direct gear linkage. Drive was taken to the rear wheels through drop-down gears and a shaft through the sump under the, thus, slightly raised engine. Although a 5-litre engine had been planned, Lamborghini business problems were to delay that for 10 years, so the 4-litre V-12 continued with 375 bhp. The body again came from Bertone's Gandini – a slender, near-single volume shape that was every bit as breath-taking as had been the Miura's. It was 5 inches wider and a shade taller, so the top speed didn't change significantly, but when it finally went into production in late 1973 as the LP400, it was well worth the wait. Unfortunately its shape had lost much of its unity in development, as the rear-mounted radiators required scoops instead of slats on the engine cover, as well as NACA ducts on the side.

Further desecration of the original shape came with the LP400S in 1978; the arrival of Pirelli's big, low profile P7 tyre brought glass-fibre eyebrows over the wheel arches, the front ones blending into a new chin-spoiler, and revised suspension. The 5-litre (4.75 actually) came in 1982 as the LP500S, but the power output remained the same but at lower revs – emission laws were biting. However the adoption of four-valves per cylinder with a 5.17-litre capacity for the LP5000S QV in 1985 raised the power to 455 bhp and the maximum speed to around 190 mph, the body remaining unchanged. And that was the final version until the Diablo arrived in 1990.

During the Countach's 16-year life, the company had endured its ups and downs, but Chrysler's take-over in 1987 gave them some stability and a chance to get on with a new car. This had a new Gandini shape, much cleaner than the Countach had become, and made good use of a greater understanding of aerodynamics above and below the car. Under the skin it remained very similar to the Countach but the space-frame was slightly lengthened to allow for the option of a four-wheel-drive version. A 5.7-litre version of the V-12 gave 492 bhp; with its more wind-cheating shape, the Diablo could reach 205 mph; the heavier 4WD VT was 3 mph slower when it arrived a year later. Since then we have had the SE30, a special edition (150-off) model to celebrate

| SPECIFICATION | MIURA P400S (1970) | COUNTACH LP400 (1975) | DIABLO (1991) |
|---|---|---|---|
| ENGINE | Ali V-12, 3929 cc | Ali V-12, 3929 cc | Ali V-12, 5707 cc |
| POWER | 370 bhp @ 7500 rpm | 375 bhp @ 8000 rpm | 492 bhp @ 7000 rpm |
| TRANSMISSION | Manual 5-speed | Manual 5-speed | Manual 5-speed |
| CHASSIS | Sheet steel | Space frame | Space frame |
| BRAKES | Discs all round | Discs all round | Discs all round |
| TOP SPEED | 172 mph | 175 mph | 205 mph |
| 0-60 MPH<br>0-100 MPH | 6.7 sec<br>15.1 sec | 5.6 sec<br>13.1 sec | 4.2 sec<br>8.5 sec |

30 years (1963-93) of Lamborghini production; this has 525 bhp and has been usefully lightened using some magnesium castings and carbon-fibre composites. You can recognise it by the slatted panel that fills in the valley behind the rear window. But even in its standard form, the Diablo is a worthy successor to the Miura.

# LANCIA AURELIA, FULVIA COUPÉ, BETA COUPÉ

*'It was a pretty little car with remarkable roadholding and ride comfort.'*

Lancia has a long history of producing cars that are never mundane and which have frequently been trend setters. Even after the Fiat take-over, the Lancia badge has adorned cars that have little obvious affinity with others in the Fiat line-up, often because Lancia has been the rallying flag-ship with such as the Stratos or Delta Integrale, following on from the traditions of the Fulvia coupé.

The history goes back to 1906 when Vincenzo Lancia founded his own company in Turin; then, as later, model names used the Greek alphabet – those that didn't had other classical connections. By 1922, he had reached the Lambda, which pioneered unitary body/chassis construction, had independent front suspension and an overhead camshaft narrow V-4. The 1937 Aprilia saloon was another trend-setter, a streamlined body, all-round independent suspension and a 1352 cc V-4 giving 47 bhp and over 80 mph – it was Vicenzo's last as he died that year, but the philosophy of innovation continued.

After the war, 1951 saw the legendary Aurelia designed by Jano (from Alfa-Romeo) and Vicenzo's son Gianni. Both saloon and the shorter B20 coupé used a new V-6 engine, initially of 1754 cc, then 1991 cc and finally of 2451 cc with 110 bhp. They also had all-round independent suspension – the pre-war sliding pillar at the front and a semi-trailing system at the rear before the latter was replaced by a de Dion axle – and a rear-mounted gearbox in unit with the final drive. The B20 was technically very advanced and offered exceptional performance, ride and roadholding for its day; it was also the first practical 2+2 style to follow on from Pininfarina's new fast-back look first shown on the 1948 Cisitalia. Over the seven years that the various versions were in production, only some 3600 coupés were built, but they performed so well on the road and in competition that many sought to emulate their stylish characteristics.

The V-6 Flaminia and front-drive flat-4 Flavia followed on with saloon and coupé variants alongside the little V-4 engined Appia which had been launched in 1953 and was replaced by the Fulvia in 1964. This came as a boxy four-door saloon or the neat and compact two-door 2+2 coupé, with a wheelbase 6.4-inches shorter.

Both used the narrow V-4 – with only 19 degrees between the banks, it used a single twin-cam cylinder head – in sizes ranging from 1100 to

*All-independent suspension, rear gearbox and a powerful V-6 engine made the Aurelia an advanced car for 1951; this 1953 B20GT shows the elegant fastback lines.*

*The Fulvia Coupé with front wheel drive was a fast and economical 2-seater that became a rally winner in 1.6HF form during the late 'sixties.*

1600 cc; this was mated to a front-drive gearbox while the wishbone front suspension was mounted on a solid sub-frame which absorbed road shocks particularly well. It was a pretty little car with remarkable roadholding and ride comfort; in its 1.6HF form it became an outright rally winner.

Good though the Lancia designs were, they were never produced in sufficient quantities to match their rivals on price and Fiat took over in 1969. The first product of the rationalisation came in 1972 with the Beta, once more front-wheel-drive but using a transversely mounted Fiat twin-cam 'four' of 1438, 1592 or 1756 cc. This came in four-door fast-back saloon form with a two-door notch-back coupé and Zagato built Spider added in 1973. The range was further extended in 1975 with the attractive and effective HPE (High Performance Estate) by which time the 1.8-litre had been superseded by a 2-litre version; at the same time came the Beta Monte Carlo. This followed the theme of the Fiat X1/9 – a mid-engined sports car using a Fiat 128 engine/transmission package – by using the Beta package still mounted transversely but behind the driver; clothed in an attractive body by Pininfarina it certainly had the looks of a mini-Ferrari but not the performance, which was why it didn't sell as well as intended. Production was suspended after 1978 but it came back again two years later and formed the basis of the Fiat group's rally

contender; although that was somewhat different under a similar skin, it kept the Monte Carlo flag flying for a few more years.

Early Betas may have had a deserved reputation for rust, but the basic design was good; the survivors are worth keeping.

*Fiat's 1969 takeover led to some rationalisation of which the Fiat-powered Beta was the first product in 1972. A coupé and the Zagato-bodied Spider came in '73, this being a 1977 2-litre coupé.*

| SPECIFICATION | AURELIA GT2500 (1955) | FULVIA COUPÉ 1.3 (1968) | BETA COUPÉ 1.8 (1976) |
|---|---|---|---|
| ENGINE | V-6 ohv, 2451 cc | V-4 dohc, 1298 cc | 4-cyl dohc, 1756 cc |
| POWER | 118 bhp @ 5000 rpm | 87 bhp @ 6000 rpm | 110 bhp @ 6000 rpm |
| TRANSMISSION | Manual 4-speed t/axle | Manual 4-speed | Manual 5-speed |
| CHASSIS | Unitary steel | Unitary steel | Unitary steel |
| BRAKES | Drums | Discs | Discs |
| TOP SPEED | 112 mph | 103 mph | 109 mph |
| 0-60 MPH | 12.3 sec | 11.9 sec | 10.7 sec |

# LOTUS SEVEN, ELITE, ELAN

*'Elans were quick cars with still exceptional road-holding and remarkable ride qualities.'*

While Lotus was a major name in *Grand Prix* circles for some 35 years, the company has been making sports cars for over 40 years. Founder Colin Chapman came up through the early post-war school of special builders, the impecunious enthusiasts who created their own competition cars around Ford or Austin 7 parts removed from tired saloons. Having built several specials and a few replicas for friends, Chapman set up his own company in 1952; his first 'production' car was the Mk.6. A clubman's competition road car, this had an aluminium body rivetted to a space-frame with a divided Ford front axle and a choice of engines. Such a clientele was quite happy to buy the car in kit form and thus avoid purchase tax.

The 7 was set to follow on, but small sports-racing cars (8, 9, 10 and 11) intervened; however, as the clubman demand was still there, the 7 was brought off the design shelves in 1957.

Using a simpler space-frame, this had wishbone front suspension and a glassfibre nose-cone, and was again a kit-car to take a variety of engines. Lotus took this through four series of progressive improvement without loss of character until the manufacturing rights were transferred to Caterham Cars in 1973; and the car is still in production although modelled now on the Series 3. However, those early Lotus sports cars were essentially small, efficient competition cars that could be used on the road, but by then Chapman wanted to produce a genuine road car.

The Elite (Lotus 14) was launched in 1957 with an innovative glassfibre monocoque shell which carried metal inserts for suspension and power train mountings and a steel roll-hoop. Producing a steel chassis was out of the question for the numbers envisaged due to high tooling costs, while space-frames would take too long to build which would make the unit cost too high. Tooling for grp (glass-reinforced plastic) was relatively cheap but it had only been used previously on unstressed bodywork; however by astute use of the various types of grp with a well-boxed structure, Chapman came up with a two-seater fixed head GT which was stiffer than most such cars. The attractive body-style came from Peter Kirwan-Taylor with aerodynamic adjustment by Frank Costin who had developed the wind-cheating sports-racers. All-round independent suspension used MacPherson strut principles which had been used on the Lotus 12, the first single-seater F2 car, together with disc brakes.

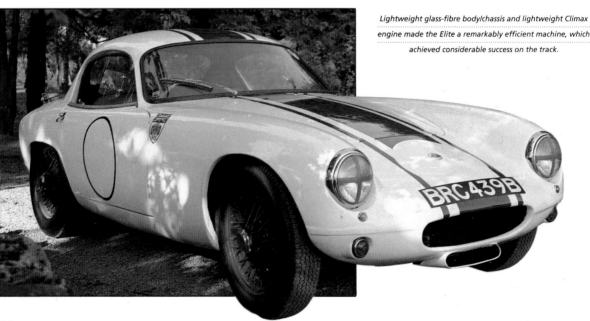

*Lightweight glass-fibre body/chassis and lightweight Climax engine made the Elite a remarkably efficient machine, which achieved considerable success on the track.*

Elite successor, the Elan was simpler to make and faster with its twin-cam 1558 cc engine. This is a Series 4 Elan.

All the Lotus cars had used small engines from Ford, BMC or the lightweight all-aluminium Coventry-Climax unit that had been developed for portable fire-pumps; Climax developed the FWE for Lotus with 1216 cc and 75 bhp. With the low drag body this was sufficient to give a 112 mph maximum rising to 117 mph when fitted with the twin carburetter 85 bhp version. With only 13.5 cwt (690 Kg) to propel, 85 bhp produced a 0-60 mph time of 10.7 seconds; it could also be very economical – 45 mpg at 70 mph – and the road-holding was exceptionally good. But despite the appeal to the keen motorist, the Elite was not a commercial success; it was not easy to make and was expensive for the performance.

For its 1962 replacement, the Elan (Lotus 26) again used glassfibre, but only for the body. The chassis was a folded sheet metal backbone with forks at each end to carry engine and front suspension and the rear suspension. Power came from the Ford-based twin-cam engine that Lotus had developed for the Lotus Cortina, with 1558 cc and 105 bhp; front suspension used normal wishbones but the rear retained the coil strut system with rubber doughnuts in the drive-shafts. The body was neat and attractive but lacked the all-time grace of the Elite. In time, it spawned the fixed head coupé (Lotus 36) and, in 1967, the stretched Elan Plus 2, the Lotus 50, arrived with reasonable rear seat space, while the engine output gradually increased to 130 bhp; although the Elans were quick cars with

| SPECIFICATION | SUPER SEVEN (1961) | ELITE SE (1962) | ELAN (1964) |
|---|---|---|---|
| ENGINE | Ford 4-cyl, 1340 cc | Ali 4-cyl, 1216 cc | Dohc 4-cyl, 1558 cc |
| POWER | 85 bhp @ 6000 rpm | 85 bhp @ 6300 rpm | 105 bhp @ 5500 rpm |
| TRANSMISSION | Manual 4-speed | Manual 4-speed | Manual 4-speed |
| CHASSIS | Steel, ali body | Grp monocoque | Steel , grp body |
| BRAKES | Drums | Discs | Discs |
| TOP SPEED | 102 mph | 117 mph | 112 mph |
| 0-60 MPH 0-100 MPH | 8.3 sec — | 10.7 sec 33.9 sec | 9.0 sec 24.1 sec |

still exceptional road-holding and remarkable ride qualities, they were still quite expensive as they were very much hand-built – as kit cars, though, without purchase tax, they were a better buy. Over 12,000 Elans and 5200 Plus 2s were built in the 12-year production run – but they served to launch Lotus as a maker of genuine road cars.

*Lotus built the 7 as a clubman's competition car, but it has remained a popular road car ever since its 1957 launch, now being produced as a Caterham 7. This is a mid-'sixties Series 2.*

# LOTUS EUROPA, ELITE, ESPRIT TURBO

*'Colin Chapman decided that Lotus should make a mid-engined replacement for the Lotus 7.'*

By the mid-'sixties Lotus was split into three operations. Lotus Cars built road cars while Team Lotus built and ran their own racing cars (including Elans and Lotus-Cortinas); Lotus Components built customer racing cars and the Lotus 7, but demand was dwindling for this side of the business. As all serious racing cars were mid-engined, Colin Chapman decided that Lotus should make a mid-engined replacement for the Lotus 7. When the Renault 16 arrived in 1964, its front-drive engine/gearbox layout seemed an ideal package for such a car. Despite their allegiance to Alpine, Renault agreed to provide 500 such units for the new Lotus 46, the Europa, which was launched in 1966.

This used what was effectively an Elan backbone chassis reversed to carry the Renault power train amidships; the engine had been uprated by Renault to give 78 bhp. Triumph front suspension assemblies and a simple rear suspension using a fixed length drive-shaft as the upper link kept costs low; as did fixed side windows and fixed seats with pedal adjustment. It had a neat enough low-drag grp body style which allowed 110 mph, but the sail panels behind the side windows obstructed visibility. By the time Lotus had finished, though, the price was nearer that of an Elan than a 7, and most of the first series went to France. An S2 followed in 1968 with such refinements as wind-up windows, a body that was no longer bonded to the backbone chassis and some luggage space behind the engine; some of these Renault-engined ones were sold in the UK, but the best version came in 1971 when the Elan's twin-cam engine was inserted with a stronger Renault gearbox, the rear panels were chopped and the interior made less stark. The final Europa Special version came in 1972 with the engine uprated to 126 bhp with a five-speed box; good for nearly 125 mph, this at last had the performance to match the chassis. Over 9000 Europas were built in the 8-year period.

Europas had also been seen on the race-tracks. Lotus Components had built 55 Lotus 47s, Europas with the twin-cam engine, for Group 4 racing during 1967. Then in 1969 a pair of Lotus 62 Europas race-proved a new engine which was to be the prototype for the new range of Lotus road cars. As the twin-cam engine needed replacement, as much for emission reasons as for the fact that it used an obsolete Ford block, Lotus had drawn up a new 2-litre 16-valve slant-4 as half of a potential future V-8; but the arrival of Vauxhall's similar Victor engine saved a lot of development time and was used with a new head and dry sump lubrication for the test-bed racers. In fact this engine was ready for production before the new Lotus cars; with Lotus' own cylinder block and 140 bhp it was used in the Jensen Healey from 1972.

The new estate-style Elite finally arrived in mid-1974 in the middle of the fuel crisis, which should have helped its sales as it was a fast, efficient four-seater with fair fuel consumption.

*Best of the Europas was the Special which used the Lotus twin-cam engine instead of the Renault 16 unit; cut down rear side panels improved visibility.*

*Under-rated, the new Elite of 1974 was an efficient 2-litre semi-estate car which should have sold well in the aftermath of the 1973 fuel crisis, but was too expensive for its performance.*

The backbone chassis principle was retained as was a refined independent suspension; Lotus' full understanding of suspension theory ensured a comfortable ride/roadholding compromise. While the body still used grp, a new Lotus process (Vacuum Assisted Resign Injection) ensured a high quality finish. For their own car, Lotus chose a 155 bhp version of the 16-valve engine which gave it a 126 mph maximum. Somehow it was never a very popular car as only 2400 had been built by the time it was phased out in 1983; even the arrival of the 2.2-litre version in 1980 hadn't helped. Meanwhile 1975 had seen the arrival of two further variations on the theme, the cheaper fastback Eclat, and the new mid-engined Esprit.

The latter had been seen at the 1972 Turin Show as a Giugiaro styling exercise on a Europa Twin-Cam chassis. Well received, it was quickly incorporated into the new range using a similar back-bone chassis design with a gearbox from the Citroen SM coupled to a 160 bhp version of the slant-4 engine. This gave it a 135 mph maximum which was enough, then, to put it near the supercar category. It finally arrived there in 1980 when the turbocharged 2.2-litre engine was adopted. In much refined form the Esprit is still in production, capable of around 160 mph.

| SPECIFICATION | EUROPA SPECIAL (1972) | ELITE (1975) | ESPRIT TURBO (1981) |
|---|---|---|---|
| ENGINE | 4-cyl dohc, 1558 cc | Ali dohc, 1973 cc | Turbo 2174 cc |
| POWER | 126 bhp @ 6500 rpm | 155 bhp @ 6500 rpm | 210 bhp @ 6000 rpm |
| TRANSMISSION | Manual 5-speed | Manual 5-speed | Manual 5-speed |
| CHASSIS | Steel backbone chassis with glassfibre bodywork (*all models*) | | |
| BRAKES | Disc/drum | Disc/drum | Discs |
| TOP SPEED | 122 mph | 126 mph | 148 mph |
| 0-60 MPH<br>0-100 MPH | 6.6 sec<br>21.6 sec | 7.8 sec<br>24.5 sec | 6.1 sec<br>17.8 sec |

*The Esprit came in 1975 but had to wait until 1980 before the Turbo took it into the supercar performance club, even if roadholding was second to very few. Two Bond films were graced with the Esprit.*

# MASERATI MISTRAL, KHAMSIN, MERAK

*'It wasn't until the factory withdrew from racing in 1957 that road cars could be taken seriously.'*

To the motor sport historian Maserati is one of the great names but, in truth, its world status really only stemmed from the mid-'fifties when the 250F ruled the *Grand Prix* scene and the sports-racing cars, 300S and 450S, were frequent front-runners although rarely winners. The company was founded in 1926 by the Maserati brothers and most of the pre-war cars were built for competition; while some of the post-war 2-litre cars were equipped with road-going bodywork, it wasn't until the factory withdrew from racing in 1957 that road cars could be taken seriously.

*This 1976 Khamsin was a product of the Citroen period of ownership. With the big V-8, the Bertone-styled 2+2 was destined for an 8-year run from 1974-82.*

For the next ten years these drew heavily on the racing designs which had mostly used six-cylinder twin-cam engines up to 3-litres, with a 4.5-litre V-8 used for that final season. However the camshafts of the road-going engines were driven by chain rather than gears, and lubrication was by wet sump systems. In fact the six-cylinder road-car engine used different dimensions within new castings, but it followed the 250F/300S design and had also been raced in the 350S. The first road car was the 3.5-litre 3500GT 2+2 which used a tubular frame under its Touring bodywork; in the days of separate chassis, coachbuilders would make single models or complete production runs. Vignale brought in the open Spider version on a

shortened chassis in 1959, the same year in which the V-8 made its first road appearance for the limited run of 32 5000GT coupés.

The six-cylinder cars received fuel injection in 1962 – 3500GTI – while 1963 saw Vignale make a coupé version of the Spider which would become the Sebring; in the same year Frua produced the Quattroporte with a 4.2-litre V-8 as well as the two-seater Mistral coupé on a further shortened 3500 chassis. By the next year this had a 3.7-litre option which would be further enlarged to 4.0-litre in 1966 when the Mistral Spider was introduced – Mistral lines are recognisable in the AC 428 which was also being built by Frua at the time. That was the last model to use the original 'six'.

The original Touring 3500 had been dropped at the end of 1964, and 1965 saw the 5000GT replaced by the Vignale-bodied Mexico, a low volume luxury four-seater powered by the V-8 in 4.2 or 4.7-litre forms. A year later came Ghia's memorable Ghibli, a supremely elegant fast-back

2-seater with the 4.7-litre V-8 (later 4.9-litre), with a spyder version following in 1968. That year Vignale added to his Mexico production with the Indy as a 4.2 or 4.7-litre four seater version of the Ghibli.

It seemed a bewildering range but Maserati just produced their chassis in different lengths with the V-8 engine in various states of tune and left most of the rest to the coachbuilders. When Citroen took over ownership in 1969, rationalisation was gradually brought in, such that by 1974 the front-engined GTs had all faded out in favour of the Bertone-bodied Khamsin 2+2 with the 4.9-litre V-8 engine. A striking looking machine, it was the first front-engined Maserati to feature independent rear suspension; it also had Citroen-style power brakes and steering assistance. The Khamsin was to stay in production until the new Biturbo range came in 1982.

Meanwhile Maserati had ventured into the mid-engined supercar field with the Bora using the 4.7-litre V-8 in a pressed steel chassis. First shown at Geneva in March 1971, this was styled by ItalDesign and was in production at Maserati by the end of the year. Strictly a two-seater, it was reasonably practical with luggage space in the front boot; and with a 160 mph potential it was

| SPECIFICATION | MISTRAL (1968) | MERAK (1973) | KHAMSIN (1978) |
|---|---|---|---|
| ENGINE | Dohc 6, 4018 cc | 4-cam V-6, 2965 cc | 4-cam V-8, 4930 cc |
| POWER | 255 bhp @ 5500 rpm | 190 bhp @ 6000 rpm | 320 bhp @ 5500 rpm |
| TRANSMISSION | Manual 5-speed | Manual 5-speed | Manual 5-speed |
| CHASSIS | Steel frame and body | Steel frame and body | Unitary steel |
| BRAKES | Discs | Discs | Discs |
| TOP SPEED | 145 mph | 140 mph | 156 mph |
| 0-60 MPH | 7.2 sec | 7.5 sec | 6.5 sec |
| 0-100 MPH | 18.4 sec | 19.9 sec | 16.8 sec |

very fast, well able to hold its head up alongside the comparable Lamborghini Miura. More practicality came with the Merak the following year; outwardly almost identical to the Bora, this used the power pack that Maserati had created for the front-drive Citroen SM – a 4-cam V-6 with transaxle mounted amidships. However as this was somewhat shorter than the V-8 plus ZF transaxle, there was room for a couple of small rear seats, or interior luggage. With only 190 bhp from the 3-litre engine, against the Bora's 310 bhp, it was considerably slower but 140 mph was fast enough for most in 1972. Three years later, the Merak SS had 220 bhp and an extra 6 mph or so.

That was the year in which Citroen retired and de Tomaso took over the reins.

*Maserati joined the mid-engined supercar league with the V-8 Bora in 1971. A year later came the Merak with the Citroen SM power train, outwardly similar but with a 2+2 configuration. The Merak SS, as this 1980 example, had 220 bhp.*

# MERCEDES 300SL, 190SL, 280SL

*'While SL had originally meant Sport Light, it had become just another model name.'*

Given Mercedes pre-war racing eminence it was hardly surprising that their post-war return to motor sport would produce something pretty special. But success was by no means guaranteed, as there was little money available in the immediate aftermath of the war to spend on expensive racing projects. When the competition 300SL appeared in 1952 it had used most of the running gear from the 300 saloons, but kept the weight down by installing it in a lightweight chassis. It was much the same philosophy that Jaguar had employed with the C-type, only that was an open car; Mercedes decided they couldn't get the outright power to win short races and that aerodynamically efficient closed cars would be faster in long distance events. Trouble was that conventional doors would cut into their space-frame chassis, so they hinged these from the roof centre and the famous gull-wing doors were born.

These new cars only raced in 1952 as the German company was too busy preparing a return to *Grand Prix* racing in 1954; but, despite their six-cylinder 3-litre engines producing less than 180 bhp, they had remarkable success – 2nd and 4th in the Mille Miglia; 1-2-3 at Bern; 1-2 at Le Mans; 1-

2-3 at Nurburgring (as open roadsters) and a final 1-2 at 102 mph in the Carrera Panamericana. Although the racing department continued to develop the cars, they didn't race again. However the American importer, Max Hoffman, insisted the company put the 300SL into production and ordered 1000; the new car was launched in February 1954, similar in overall design to the racing coupés, but incorporating some of the later developments, such as the Bosch fuel injection system which lifted the power to 200 bhp – when equipped with the sports camshaft this rose to 220 bhp.

Capable of around 145 mph, it became the instant supercar of the day and continued to be successful in competition, racing and rallying. By the time the coupé was phased out in favour of the roadster in 1957, nearly 1400 had been built; the open car retained the space-frame but conventional deeper doors were fitted. The new car also adopted the low-pivot swing axle of the later saloons; the normal swing axle used at the rear of the coupé had given it a rather tail-happy reputation.

Meanwhile part of Hoffman's proposal had been for a smaller sports car; the 190SL roadster

*Conceived as the little brother to the 300SL, the 190SL looked very similar but its 4-cylinder engine produced only 105 bhp against the bigger car's 200 bhp.*

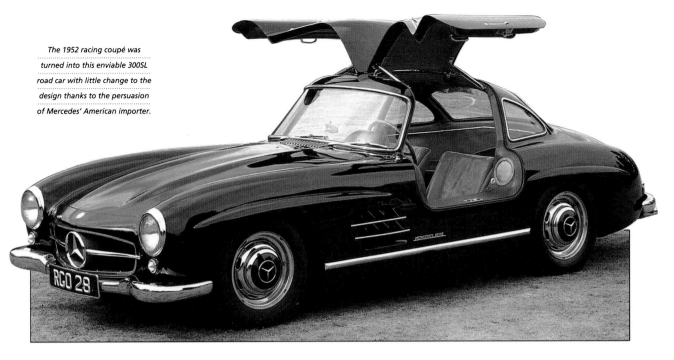

was launched at the same time as the 300SL. Outwardly very similar to the later 300SL roadster, this had a conventional saloon car platform with a 1.9-litre four-cylinder developing 105 bhp which was enough for around 110 mph. While it lacked the charisma of its bigger brother, it was a successful model in its own right.

The two roadsters stayed in production until 1963 when they were replaced by the 230SL, based on a shortened version of the 220SE saloon, but with its own distinctive styling. While SL had originally meant Sport Light, it had become just another model name; although all subsequent SLs were sportier and lighter than the saloons from which they were derived, they were fully engineered Mercedes road cars with no competition intention. The 230SL was a 2-seater roadster but could be fitted with a substantial hard-top which turned it into a properly trimmed coupé for winter use – it needed at least two people to remove this elegant pagoda-style roof. With 150 bhp from the 2.3-litre six-cylinder, the 230SL was a 120 mph car, or 115 mph when fitted with the more popular Mercedes 4-speed automatic transmission. Some 20,000 cars later, 1966 saw the 250SL with the same 150 bhp but more torque; another 5000 models on and a year later came the 280SL, still basically the same car but the 2.8-litre six-cylinder now produced 170 bhp which added another 5 mph. This SL range

came to an end in 1971. The replacements were very similar but were mostly based on the new V-8 engines, rising to the flagship 500SL in 1985. The current range came in 1989, and like all the SLs are assured of future classic status.

| SPECIFICATION | 300SL (1955) | 190SL (1956) | 280SL (1968) |
|---|---|---|---|
| ENGINE | Six-cyl, 2996 cc | Four-cyl, 1897 cc | Six-cyl, 2778 cc |
| POWER | 220 bhp @ 5800 rpm | 105 bhp @ 5700 rpm | 170 bhp @ 5500 rpm |
| TRANSMISSION | Manual 4-speed | Manual 4-speed | Auto 4-speed |
| CHASSIS | Steel frame, ali body | Unitary steel | Unitary steel |
| BRAKES | Drums | Drums | Discs |
| TOP SPEED | 145 mph | 109 mph | 121 mph |
| 0-60 MPH 0-100 MPH | 7.2 sec 16.2 sec | 13.3 sec — | 9.3 sec 25.8 sec |

# MG TC, TD, TF

*The MG TC (red car) took the British sports car into America. Small, agile and fun, it gave the visiting GIs a taste for the open air. Successor to the TC, the TD (green car) brought the front suspension up to date with independent wishbones within the still square-rigged shape.*

While the MG had catered for a very British clientele before the 1939-45 war, the TC was to launch the marque on the world market, thanks in large part to the war. Many of Britain's allied troops had met the little British sports car at that time and fallen in love with it; Americans particularly, accustomed to larger, less sporting machinery, welcomed a car that made motoring enjoyable. To them it was also a natural successor to the Jeep in which many of them had their first experience of sporting motoring.

The initials MG came from Morris Garages, the retail off-shoot of William Morris' Oxford-based factory which had started producing cars in 1913. Cecil Kimber, the father of MG, was the manager of Morris Garages and, in the early 'twenties, decided to produce sporting versions of the Morris Cowley. Thus was born the marque MG. Then, as now, much of its content came from other mass-production models within the same company.

The MG TC was launched in 1945. In fact it was little changed from the TB which had been announced in 1939, but very few were built before the outbreak of war – just 379. And the TB had been the successor to the TA, launched as the T-type in 1936, with the customary MG soubriquet of Midget which had endorsed many of the previous models. The TA had been powered by a version of the Wolseley engine, a four-cylinder 1292 cc unit developing 52 bhp. For the TB this had been changed for the stronger, and potentially more tuneable, Morris engine; although slightly smaller at 1250 cc it developed 54 bhp with its twin SU carburetters.

Came the end of the war and a return to car production, MG abandoned their multi-model policy and concentrated all efforts on the new TC with just a single two-seater body-style. With little time available for development, design changes were kept to a minimum; the cramped cockpit was made four inches wider and the rear spring design was changed for more simple maintenance. So the TC was put quickly into production at a time when most manufacturers were still struggling to get going again.

So the TC was basically a pre-war design and looked it. The chassis was a simple box-section ladder with its axles carried on semi-elliptic springs. It wasn't fast even by period standards – 75 mph flat out and 15 seconds to reach 50 mph. But what it had was charisma. Wire wheels, long bonnet, big radiator grille and slab petrol tank exposed at the back, it looked like everyone's sporting ideal. It rapidly became MG's biggest volume model ever and 10,000 were made by the time it ceased late in 1949; one third stayed in Britain and 2000 went to America.

Pre-war in looks, the TC was also pre-war in road behaviour. Stiff springing gave an uncomfortable ride and poor, if entertaining, roadholding on poor surfaces. The TD was to change that – if not the performance. In 1947, MG had introduced the Y-type saloon; it had a slightly different chassis from that of the TC, but that carried independent front suspension. The TD made use of a shortened version of the Y-type chassis which brought the added benefit of increased track for better roadholding; this was further enhanced by lower, fatter tyres, now 5.50 x 15 instead of 4.50 x 19. The extra width, length and the introduction of bumpers served to add weight, so the same engine made the TD less accelerative than the TC – but it looked more modern and had the right appeal. Nearly 30,000 were sold during its four-year life and the majority were exported.

By 1953, though, demand was falling; the TD was looking old-fashioned and it was slow compared with the new Austin-Healey 100 introduced in late 1952. That was a product of the same BMC, and MG were not allowed to produce another all-new sports car for the same market. The best they could achieve was the TF, a face-lifted TD, lower with a sloping dummy radiator grille, more comfortable and heavier; while its rakish lines increased the appeal, the performance was even slower than that of the TD. In 1954, the insertion of a 1466 cc version of the same engine, increased the power to 63 bhp and sustained some demand for the final year of T-series production – the more modern MGA was launched in late 1955.

Over its 19-year span, the T-series gave International fame to the name of MG. Many racing drivers cut their track teeth on the cars and they embodied all that was best in traditional British sporting machinery, dated though they had become by 1955. Their classic appeal has never diminished.

*Last of the T-series, the TF was a belated attempt to bring a modern look to an old style. The 1500 cc engine finally added some performance in the year after this 1953 car.*

*'Americans welcomed a car that made motoring enjoyable.'*

| SPECIFICATION | MG TC (1948) | MG TD Mk.II (1952) | MG TF 1500 (1954) |
|---|---|---|---|
| ENGINE | 4-cyl 1250 cc | 4-cyl 1250 cc | 4-cyl 1466 cc |
| HORSEPOWER | 54 bhp @ 5200 rpm | 57 bhp @ 5500 rpm | 63 bhp @ 5000 rpm |
| TRANSMISSION | 4-speed manual | 4-speed manual | 4-speed manual |
| CHASSIS | Steel box frame with separate body panels (*all models*) | | |
| BRAKES | Hydraulically operated drum brakes all round (*all models*) | | |
| TOP SPEED | 75 mph | 77 mph | 80 mph |
| 0-60 MPH | 22.7 sec | 23.9 sec | 19.5 sec |

# MGA, MGB, MGC

*'It was just what the market wanted with near 100 mph performance, good roadholding and attractive modern styling.'*

Despite the fact that MG was Britain's traditional sports car, the BMC management of the day nearly let the marque die in the early 'fifties. The T-series cars were looking very old-fashioned, but no-one would sanction the development of the special-bodied MG TD that had been built for Le Mans in 1951; BMC were going to launch the new Austin-Healey 100 at the 1952 Motor Show and didn't need two new sports cars. The TF face-lift was all that was allowed, but the Triumph TR2, which arrived at the same 1953 Show, was another nail in the T-series coffin.

The Y-type MG saloon had likewise been getting a little long in the tooth. This was partially cured with the 1953 launch of the ZA Magnette. This followed on from the Wolseley 4/44 which had been launched the year before using the MG TD's 1250 cc engine, but the MG received the new BMC B-series 1489 cc unit – the Wolseley would get the same engine in 1956 and become the 15/50. The ZA and its ZB successor went on to be highly regarded sports saloons.

While that 1951 Le Mans MG had sat at Abingdon, the new chief engineer, Syd Enever, had made a new chassis which allowed the occupants to sit lower in the same body than had been possible with the TD chassis. While this had

been completed in 1952 using the TF 1500 engine, and had been converted to a possible record car in 1953, it wasn't until mid-1954 that Enever was given the order to turn this into a production reality and to use the new B-series engine with 68 bhp. Three prototypes were entered in the 1955 Le Mans 24-hours and two finished, one averaging 86 mph; still as prototypes, three ran in the TT that year and one finished 4th in class behind the Porsches. Finally the MGA was announced for the 1955 Show with an instant competition history. It was just what the market wanted with near 100 mph performance, good roadholding and attractive modern styling – it rapidly outsold all previous MGs. A year later the roadster was joined by the fixed head coupé and in 1958 both became available with a 1588 cc 108 bhp twin-cam engine. The MGA 1600 came in 1959 with 80 bhp and disc front brakes, while the final version from 1961 was the 93 bhp 1622 cc Mk.II 1600. Just over 100,000 MGAs were produced in the 1955-62 period, more than twice the post-war T-series over 1945-55.

MGB production figures were even more impressive; over half a million were to be produced over the next 18 years before the Abingdon factory closed for ever. Higher volumes were always

*Although the MGA was late to join the mid-range sports car market in 1955, it soon became a very popular car. The example shown is the rare Twin Cam, easily distinguished by its Dunlop knock-off wheels.*

envisaged for the MGA's replacement, so the separate body/chassis construction of the A gave way to the monocoque construction of the B. The power unit was still the trusty B-series now enlarged to 1798 cc and 95 bhp while the 4-speed gearbox could be supplemented with an overdrive. The new sports car was considerably more comfortable than its predecessor with more space as well as a better ride; and it could comfortably clear 100 mph too. As before, the roadster was joined by a coupé, the MGB GT, in 1966. Over the years there was little apparent change to the basic B, apart from the switch from chrome to rubber bumpers, but a host of detail changes came in response to changing safety and emission legislation; and there were two short-lived additional models.

It was safety legislation that was terminating big Healey production. A six-cylinder MGB should have been a suitable replacement. Unfortunately the 3-litre engine chosen for the MGC in 1967 was a particularly gutless and overweight unit developed for the Austin 3-litre saloon; its size and weight caused a front suspension redesign and the handling became most unsporting – it was somewhat better with the GT version which had stiffer rear springs. It actually needed very little work to make the GT into a worthy Healey replacement – better engine breathing and a shorter axle ratio – but this was never done by MG and the model died after just two years and 9000 cars.

| SPECIFICATION | MGA 1500 (1955) | MGB (1962) | MGC GT (1967) |
|---|---|---|---|
| ENGINE | 4-cyl, 1489 cc | 4-cyl, 1798 cc | 6-cyl, 2912 cc |
| POWER | 68 bhp @ 5500 rpm | 95 bhp @ 5400 rpm | 145 bhp @ 5250 rpm |
| TRANSMISSION | Manual 4-speed | Manual 4-speed | Manual 4-speed + o/d |
| CHASSIS | Steel chassis/body | Unitary steel | Unitary steel |
| BRAKES | Drums | Disc/drum | Disc/drum |
| TOP SPEED | 98 mph | 108 mph | 119 mph |
| 0-60 MPH | 16.0 sec | 12.1 sec | 10.1 sec |

The other short-term model was the MGB GT V-8; somewhat belatedly the 3.5-litre Rover V-8 was fitted to the GT to provide a very rapid sports coupé from 1972-6, but it was canned after only 2591 had been built, reputedly because Rover needed all the engines for their other products. Maybe the old B design was dated by the mid-'seventies, but the 125 mph B GT V-8 gave very good performance value.

*The MGB was designed for big numbers and half a million were produced over 18 years. The GT came in 1966, and the MGBGT V-8 shown here started its short-lived run in 1972.*

*Conceived as a replacement for the big Healey, the MGC had a gutless six-cylinder engine and poor handling. However, intelligent tuning could transform them into proper sports cars, like this 1968 rally version.*

# MORGAN 4/4, PLUS 4, PLUS 8

*'The Morgan is essentially a 'thirties classic with performance that keeps pace with the times.'*

Founded in 1910, the Morgan Motor Company spent its first twenty-five years making three-wheelers, the stable kind with two front wheels set wide apart. They ranged from runabouts to competition speed models, the engines from twin-cylinder air-cooled to four-cylinder water-cooled. Their success was based on sound engineering. What is particularly remarkable is that the first model had an independent front suspension design which is still in use on present-day Morgans – the sliding pillar system.

The first four-wheeler came in 1936; the 4/4 denoted four wheels and a four-cylinder engine, an 1122 cc side-valve Coventry Climax; its design set the pattern that was to follow. Where most used a channel section chassis, Morgan used a Z-section which made it easier to mount the floorboards; at the front was the familiar sliding pillar suspension, while the rear saw a conventional live axle mounted on underslung leaf springs which were inset from the chassis side members. The four-speed Moss gearbox was distanced from the engine by a short tube to ensure that the gear lever could act directly on the selectors without a long lever or remote control. The steel bodywork was mounted on ash

frames with contemporary styling – long louvred bonnet with chrome radiator, front wings sweeping into running boards, and twin spare wheels mounted on the flat tail. It was a sleek modern motor car back in 1936 with a maximum speed of almost 80 mph.

Since then, little has changed in the style. The flat radiator gave way to a cowled one in 1954 when the headlights were fared into the wings, while the body is wider than it used to be. A four-seater version was offered in 1937 and is still available. Over the years it is only changing power units that have denoted the different models; although some of the design features have been strengthened and the chassis length has also varied, the Morgan is essentially a 'thirties classic with performance that keeps pace with the times thanks to period engines.

The 34 bhp Climax engine was supplemented with an overhead valve Standard Flying Ten unit of 1267 cc with 39 bhp in 1939. After the war, Morgan continued with the Standard-powered 4/4 while the 3-wheelers were to remain in production using side-valve Ford units until 1950. When Standard decided to use just a single engine

*Initially with the Vanguard 2088 cc 'four', the Plus 4 stuck to Triumph TR power through to 1968. This 1966 4-seater uses the TR4's 2138 cc engine.*

When the TR5 adopted a six-cylinder engine, Morgan switched to the Rover V-8 to create the Plus 8 which has been the mainstay from 1968 onwards.

for the new Vanguard, Morgan moved with them and adopted the big 2088 cc 68 bhp four-cylinder in 1951 to create the Plus 4. An improved 1991 cc version of this engine was created for the TR2 in 1953 with 90 bhp, but it wasn't until 1955 that Morgan were allowed to use it, and then only in limited quantities; accordingly Morgan brought back the 4/4 range using the side-valve 1172 cc Ford engine and gearbox as the 4/4 Series 2 – with the same power as the pre-war models it is not surprising that the top speed didn't change from 75 mph but it was a popular car. When the 100 bhp TR3 engine was fitted to the Plus 4 from 1956, Morgan had a genuine 100 mph car; Motor's 1957 road test was headed 'A modern vintage sports car with vivid acceleration' . . . but they liked it!

The Plus 4 would continue with the TR engines until the arrival of the six-cylinder TR5 made them obsolete; fortunately for Morgan enthusiasts the six wouldn't fit, but Rover's 3.5-litre V-8 could be shoe-horned in with small increases in chassis length and width; still mated to a Moss gearbox which had been strengthened over the years, the new Plus 8 arrived in 1968 and has been the backbone of production ever since – with 168 bhp it became an instant 125 mph car and could reach 100 mph in under 20 seconds. Still primitive in the comfort department, it was and has remained great fun.

Meanwhile the 4/4 had become a Series 3 using the Ford 997 cc ohv engine in 1961, changing to a Series 4 a year later with the 1340 cc version and a Series 5 with the 1498 cc Ford in 1963. That year saw Morgan's only attempt to modernise the range with a neat two-seater glassfibre coupé body placed on top of the Plus 4 chassis; it was not a success and only 50 were made.

Throughout Morgan existence the cars have been regularly used in competitions, from trials and rallies to circuit racing. The most famous success was with a competition version of the Plus 4 in the 1962 Le Mans 24-hour race; finishing 13th overall, it won the 2-litre class. Today's Morgans are just as much at home on road and track as their predecessors.

The original 4/4 was Morgan's first four-wheeler. Subsequent 4/4 series cars started again in 1955 with Ford power, from the 1172 cc side-valve to the 1498 cc Cortina unit in 1963. This is a 1972 4/4.

| SPECIFICATION | 4/4 SERIES 2 (1956) | PLUS 4 (1957) | PLUS 8 (1968) |
|---|---|---|---|
| ENGINE | Ford sv, 1172 cc | Triumph ohv, 1991 cc | Rover V-8, 3528 cc |
| POWER | 36 bhp @ 4400 rpm | 100 bhp @ 4800 rpm | 168 bhp @ 5200 rpm |
| TRANSMISSION | Manual 3-speed | Manual 4-speed | Manual 4-speed |
| CHASSIS | Cross-braced Z-section steel chassis with steel bodywork (all models) | | |
| BRAKES | Drums | Drums | Disc/drum |
| TOP SPEED | 75 mph | 100 mph | 125 mph |
| 0-60 MPH / 0-100 MPH | 26.9 sec / — | 9.7 sec / — | 6.7 sec / 19.0 sec |

71

# NISSAN 240Z, 280ZX TURBO, 300ZX

'With 150 bhp it was a 125 mph car which could reach 100 mph in 24 seconds.'

Arriving in 1969 as the Datsun 240Z, Nissan's all-independently sprung GT coupé, powered by an overhead-cam 2.4-litre six, was the spiritual successor to the big Healey in the eyes of most enthusiasts. It was what the next Healey should have been and made a mockery of the short-lived MGC; it was designed for the American market as a more affordable alternative to Porsches and the Jaguar E; backed by competition success, it received great acclaim – over 156,000 were built in its four-year life with the majority going to America.

The project had actually started in 1963 when Nissan commissioned Yamaha to create a mini E-type from scratch. This was achieved by the end of 1964 using a body style that had been drawn up by Albrecht Goertz – renowned for the BMW 507 of the previous decade. For whatever reason, Nissan did not take this up, so Yamaha offered it to Toyota who turned it into the 2000GT which was announced at the 1965 Tokyo Motor Show. Nissan then returned to the idea two years later and came up with the 240Z which was launched in 1969.

This used a unitary construction coupé body incorporating various components from other Nissan/Datsun models. The six-cylinder engine used moving parts from the 4-cylinder Bluebird, the gearbox came from the 2000 Sports and the MacPherson front suspension from the Laurel saloon; struts were also used for the independent rear. Using carefully chosen high volume components for a low volume niche car was what MG had done for years, but Nissan were able to capitalise on the system just at the moment that MG faltered. With 150 bhp it was a 125 mph car which could reach 100 mph in 24 seconds. Competition successes included two consecutive US SCCA Production championships and victories in the East African Safari rally in 1971 and 1973 – it was tough as well as fast.

However, increasingly stringent American safety and emission legislation were beginning to slow the car down with restricted power and more weight. The 260Z went some way towards restoring the balance in 1974, at which point a 2+2 was introduced with an extra 12-inches in the wheelbase. A year later, another engine stretch brought the 280Z with fuel injection but it was still not as accelerative as the original 240Z, which was 250Kg lighter. There was no way that Nissan could go back to the original sports car concept without an all-new design, so they deserted that section of the market and headed for the luxury personal car sector with the 280ZX in 1978.

Although similar in style, the ZX was largely new, and featured a semi-trailing arm rear suspension; the 2.8-litre injection engine was carried over but 140 bhp pushing 2800 lb was a poor comparison with the 240Z's 150 bhp and 2300 lb; a better shape kept the maximum speed up to 121 mph though. In 1980, the 2-seater and 2+2 were supplemented with the T-bar roof version with a pair of removable smoked glass panels, an option which accounted for over half the US sales in 1980. Finally in 1981 came a Z-car

*Sporting fast-back style, independent rear suspension, free-revving ohc 'six' – it was just what Healey fans wanted to replace the aging 3000. Datsun gave it to them with the successful 240Z.*

that was faster than the original; a turbocharger took the output up to 180 bhp lifting the maximum speed up to 129 mph; improved steering and suspension with bigger tyres also made it a nicer car with some of the sporting appeal restored. It was the last sports car to use the Datsun name.

Only two years later came the first Nissan 300ZX. The engine this time was a two-cam 3-litre V-6 in normally aspirated 170 bhp and turbocharged 225 bhp forms, the American turbo version having 205 bhp. While this was essentially a revamped 280ZX, the body panels were all new and the shape considerably cleaner – the European cars would reach 140 mph; further shape revisions would take place in 1987.

The new 300ZX came in 1989 and was packed with hi-tech equipment, from variable valve timing on the 24-valve V-6 to HICAS rear steering on its multi-link independent suspension. In normally aspirated form the engine developed 222 bhp, which is enough for 143 mph and 0-60 mph in 6.7 seconds; but the twin turbo version developed 300 bhp (280 bhp for low octane Europe) and will reach 155 mph with a 0-60 mph time of 5.6 seconds. Americans can have two-seater versions but the European market has the 2+2 with an extra 4.7 inches in the wheelbase.

The 300ZX is an extremely effective sports coupé which has earned as passionate a following as did the old 240Z of twenty years earlier.

*The 280ZX, pictured here, moved further in the comfort direction.*

| SPECIFICATION | 240Z (1969) | 280ZX TURBO (1986) | 300ZX (1990) |
|---|---|---|---|
| ENGINE | 6-cyl, 2393 cc | 6-cyl, 2753 cc | V-6, dohc, 2960 cc |
| POWER | 150 bhp @ 5600 rpm | 180 bhp @ 5600 rpm | 300 bhp @ 6400 rpm |
| TRANSMISSION | Manual 5-speed | Manual 5-speed | Manual 5-speed |
| CHASSIS | Unitary steel | Unitary steel | Unitary steel |
| BRAKES | Disc/drum | Discs | Discs with ABS |
| TOP SPEED | 125 mph | 129 mph | 155 mph |
| 0-60 MPH<br>0-100 MPH | 8.3 sec<br>23.9 sec | 7.9 sec<br>20.5 sec | 5.6 sec<br>14.9 sec |

*While the 1983 300ZX was a recognisable descendant of the 240Z, the 1989 300ZX was full of the latest Nissan technology under a completely new skin.*

# PONTIAC GTO, FIREBIRD TRANS-AM, FIERO

*'The youth market was all about performance.'*

Pontiac always seems to retain more autonomy than most GM divisions, in style as well as fundamental engineering; high performance packs have been part of the option list since the division found its feet in the late 'fifties under Bunkie Knudsen. Knudsen recognised that the youth market was all about performance, whether on the race track or the drag-strip; they went racing. Between 1957 and 1963, Pontiac saloons won 69 top NASCAR races, including three Daytona 500s on the trot in 1957-9. In the showrooms every purchase form had a massive list of option boxes to convert a staid base model into a high-style road-racer.

However in 1963 GM put a stop to factory racing and option boxes seemed set to diminish rapidly. The Pontiac response was to follow the hot-rodders' dictum of dropping a large engine into a small car. The chosen recipient was the 1964 Tempest, a conventional car until you reached the end of the option list and found the GTO pack. Pontiac had already started down the route of race-evocative name tags like *Grand Prix* and *Le Mans*, so borrowing the Ferrari GT soubriquet caused no heartache in Detroit. The GTO pack was based on the 389 cu.in (6.4-litre) V-8 fitted to the bigger and heavier Catalina and Bonneville ranges; it came in 325 and 348 bhp forms with a stiffer suspension and the famous lettering set into the grille and on the flanks – Ferrari never did that!

While the car was technically a Tempest GTO and most were fitted to the Le Mans coupé and convertible, the GTO option was also available for the four-door and the estate. Despite GM management reservations, the GTO was an instant success; plans to produce just 5000 were swamped and 32,000 were sold in that first year. The muscle car had arrived, and option packs were back with a vengeance. For 1965, the base GTO was given 335 bhp with 360 bhp as the alternative using triple twin-choke carburetters. The following year saw a new style with a fast-back joining the convertible and hard-top, but the car was getting heavy; for 1967 the engine was bored out to 400 cu.in but still with 360 bhp on a single four-barrel carb – a 4-bolt-mains block came in mid-year as part of the ram-air package with scoops on the bonnet.

An innovative plastic bumper-less front end characterised the 1968 cars which also had disappearing headlights set into the grille; 1969 saw the arrival of the orange Judge, complete with 400 cu.in. 355 bhp engine with a rev counter on

*Just a number on the Tempest option list, the GTO was the first of the auto-makers' muscle cars to follow hot-rod practice and put the biggest engine into the smallest car – this is a 1966 model.*

Pontiac's attempt to make an American Fiat X1/9 as a personal commuter car met with little success.

the back of the bonnet. By 1970 the top engine was up to 455 cu.in (7.45-litres), still with 360 bhp. Ever more strangled by emission legislation, the GTO carried on until 1973, by which time the pony-car market was in full swing (see also Mustang – page 44).

Chevrolet had introduced the Camaro in autumn 1966 and Pontiac's Firebird, always the better looking, followed in early 1967. Pontiac didn't join in the pony programme until the beginning of 1966, so used the Camaro centre section with its own front and rear. The engine choice ran from the 230 cu.in (3.8-litre) six with 165 bhp, through the 250 cu.in 'six' and the 326 cu.in (5.3-litre) 250 bhp V-8, to the top of the range 400 cu.in (6.6-litres) developing 325 bhp. By 1966, Mustang lessons had been thoroughly absorbed, and there was a full list of options including manual boxes and the GM 2 and 3-speed automatics.

Despite Pontiac's sporting past, it was Chevrolet who went racing. Using the 5-litre 302 Z-28 option, Roger Penske took the Camaro to two consecutive Trans-Am championships in 1968/9, but it was Pontiac who took the model name and the Firebird Trans-Am has been top of the range ever since. While early Firebirds looked very European, the 'nineties range has had a global attraction that outshines most; paint a 1995 Trans-Am Ferrari red and Pininfarina would get the applause.

By the end of the 'seventies, Pontiac orders were not too strong and they were seeking to rejoin the youth market. Ever innovative, they came up with the mid-engined Fiero, similar in concept to the Fiat X1/9. To GM, sports cars meant Corvette, so the Fiero was only allowed to be called a commuter car and was initially given a basic four-cylinder 2.5-litre lump with a mere 92 bhp taken from a front-wheel-drive car. It used a basic steel sub-frame but every external panel was in some form of plastic. Launched in September 1983, it was given a 2.8-litre V-6 option with 140 bhp for 1985 which gave it the 125 mph performance its chassis deserved. It was probably too small for the American roads and never gained a great following, despite providing the basis for an IMSA race-derivative. In 1988 it was dropped, a sadly short run for an enterprising design.

Below: Pontiac's Firebird was the pair for the Chevrolet Camaro, but it was the Firebird that used the Trans-Am title for the top of the range. Plastic noses were well established by the time of this 1979 Trans-Am.

| SPECIFICATION | GTO (1964) | FIREBIRD T-A (1969) | FIERO (1986) |
|---|---|---|---|
| ENGINE | Cast-iron V-8, 6377 cc | Cast-iron V-8, 6550 cc | Cast-iron V-6, 2837 cc |
| POWER | 325 bhp @ 4800 rpm | 335 bhp @ 5000 rpm | 135 bhp @ 4900 rpm |
| TRANSMISSION | Manual 4-speed | Auto 3-speed | Manual 5-speed |
| CHASSIS | Perimeter frame | Unitary steel | Steel & plastic |
| BRAKES | Drums | Discs all round | Discs all round |
| TOP SPEED | 122 mph | 125 mph | 125 mph |
| 0-60 MPH | 6.9 sec | 5.8 sec | 7.7 sec |

# PORSCHE SPEEDSTER, SUPER 75, 1600SC

*'The tail happy handling had gradually been brought under reasonable control.'*

Although Dr. Porsche had a remarkable reputation in the automotive engineering world for most of the first half of the century, the man in the street knew nothing of the name until the mid-'fifties, by which time a few of the aerodynamic coupés were spread around the world – the 5000th car emerged from the Zuffenhausen plant in March 1954. Ten years later, the 911 would commence the rise to iconic status.

Dr Porsche's first project at the turn of the century was the electric Lohner-Porsche in his native Austria. He then worked with Austro-Daimler before joining the parent company in Stuttgart for whom he developed the powerful open Mercedes-Benz sports cars. With his own consultancy during the 'thirties, he was the man behind the Auto-Union GP car and the designer of the Volkswagen Beetle. As competition was a Porsche watchword, he designed and built three VW coupés to take part in a Berlin-Rome road race which the war cancelled.

This design, using the characteristic rear-mounted air-cooled engine and Beetle suspension components, was to form the basis of Porsche production which started in 1948. While the first of these 356s was an open car, the rest would be coupés until the Cabriolet joined the range in 1951; by this time only 50 cars had been built during two years in Austria before the move to Stuttgart generated an increase to 60 cars per month. Those original 356s used an 1100 cc version of the Beetle's flat-four engine giving out all of 40 bhp; but the aerodynamic shape allowed a top speed over 80 mph.

In 1951 the engine was enlarged to 1300 cc and 44 bhp, while a new roller-bearing 1500 cc unit with aluminium heads became top of the range with 60 bhp and a 95 mph performance capability. Porsche was on the power ladder; while the cars changed little, extra power justified a model change. The 1300S came in 1953 and the 1500S with 70 bhp followed a year later.

Already Porsches were beginning to record

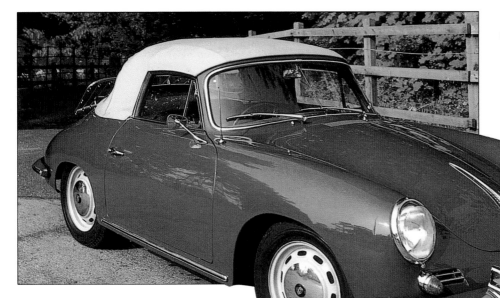

Cabriolets joined the range in 1951 with a more substantial roof than the Speedster or later Roadster.

class victories in International motor sport; at Le Mans they won the 1100 cc class from 1951-55 and the 1500 cc class from 1953-55. Class wins from 1952-54 in the Mexican Carrera Panamericana justified the name Carrera being applied to the top of the Porsche range in 1955. Competition would always be used to promote the Porsche name.

While the Cabriolet had been offered in 1951, the American market wanted a cheaper open Porsche with a simpler folding roof; the result was the 1952 America model which led directly to the 1954 Speedster. Although this was still a cabriolet below the waistline, the windscreen was 3.5 inches shorter, which gave the car a much lower-looking appearance. The Speedster and the Roadster would become interchangeable with Convertible D through to 1963.

The first major change to the appearance of the 356 came in 1956 with the 356A featuring a curved windscreen, wider 15-inch wheels, a new painted bumper style and a 1600 cc engine option plus a few interior changes. This mixture of engineering and minor styling changes would produce the 356B in 1960 and the 356C in 1963. By then the rear window had been considerably enlarged, disc brakes were used on all four wheels and the engine choice was limited to 1600 cc in 75 bhp C and 95 bhp SC forms. The tail happy handling had gradually been brought under reasonable control. The final 1600SC was an

impressive sporting car that had diverged a long way from its Beetle ancestor over the intervening 15 years.

The final 356C series came in 1963 with disc brakes all round, and engine options of 75 or 90 bhp.

| SPECIFICATION | 1500 SPEEDSTER (1956) | SUPER 75 (1960) | 1600SC (1964) |
|---|---|---|---|
| ENGINE | Air-cooled flat-4 1488 cc or 1582 cc | | |
| HORSEPOWER | 66 bhp @ 4400 rpm | 75 bhp @ 5000 rpm | 95 bhp @ 5800 rpm |
| TRANSMISSION | Manual 4-speed (all models) | | |
| CHASSIS | Steel unitary body/chassis (all models) | | |
| BRAKES | Drums | Drums | Discs |
| TOP SPEED | 100 mph | 110 mph | 115 mph |
| 0-60 MPH | 13.9 sec | 14.6 sec | 13.2 sec |

# PORSCHE 911, 911S 2.4, 911 TURBO 3.0

By the time the Porsche 911 arrived in 1963, the name had become as well known around the race-tracks of the world as it was in the high streets and over 76,000 had been produced in the 15-year life of the 356. The 911 was really an evolution from the 356 in that the rear-mounted air-cooled engine layout remained the same, and the basic design was laid out by the same people who had drawn up the original car.

But the Beetle no longer provided any parts. The new engine was an air-cooled flat-6 2-litre which developed 130 bhp; as before, the rear mounting allowed an aerodynamically clean front end, and the car would do 130 mph. The rear seats would take slightly older children than in a 356 and they still folded flat to increase the luggage capacity, which was already good with the whole of the front compartment available.

*Thirty years ago, the 911 was a clean, lithe shape with no air dams, wheel-arch flares or rear wings. With 130 bhp from 2-litres giving 130 mph it was very efficient in every way. S-type wheels were an early option.*

Maybe its heating and ventilation was primitive, maybe you had to drive with care in the wet, but this was a driver's car, and one that would keep going and going.

The Targa version, launched in 1965, has been with us almost as long; in design it appears to follow the Triumph TR4's Surrey top – a lift-out panel held between fixed front and rear screens – but Porsche made the vertical pillar into a safety roll-over bar, and it has been a model option ever since; a full folding-roof Cabriolet was only added in 1982.

First in the series of steady uprates came in 1967 with the 911S sporting the famous five-spoke alloy wheels; the 2-litre engine was uprated to 160 bhp. A year later, the wheelbase was stretched by 2.2 inches to improve the weight distribution, and the body flared to allow wider rear wheels. Three

While the roadholding characteristics of the 356 could easily catch out the unwary with a sudden tail-slide, just like the VW Beetle, the 911 design attempted to tame this with revised rear suspension, but this was only partially successful. The 911 would always be potentially tail-happy until the arrival of the four wheel drive versions. However, few people drive on the limit and the 911 was a success from the moment it arrived.

different engine versions ranged from the 911T at 110 bhp through the 140 bhp 911E to the 911S, now with fuel injection and 170 bhp. In 1970 these three models remained the same, but all engines were now 2.2-litre, and two years later the capacity went to 2341 cc – nominal 2.4 – with the three outputs at 130 bhp, 165 bhp and 190 bhp, the last capable of 147 mph.

Some of this steady capacity increase was to offset the restrictions of exhaust emission legislation without losing performance. For 1974 Porsche introduced the American 5 mph bumpers across the range and increased the capacity to the 2.7-litres which the Carrera RS had sported the previous year. A considerable programme of refinement had been effected too, including a better heating system, more comfortable seats and headlamp washers. This all left the 911S 2.7 down on power at 167 bhp but improved torque from the latest Bosch injection system ensured this was hardly noticeable. Besides, there was the Carrera RS now with 3-litres, and in 1975 the Turbo would arrive to expand the range.

The 911s had always done well in GT classes in the hands of private racers, but new International racing rules for 1976 gave a chance of outright victory to derivatives of road cars. Porsche had gained considerable experience of turbocharging when racing the Can-Am 917/30; it was logical to put this to good effect and create a race-winning 911 with turbocharging. But you have to sell road-going versions of such GT racers, so the 3-litre Turbo was launched in 1975 with 260 bhp.

The 911 cult and engine capacity continued to grow and they will all be recognised as classics in time; our selection comes from 20 years back.

| SPECIFICATION | 911 (1963) | 911S 2.4 (1972) | TURBO 3.0 (1975) |
|---|---|---|---|
| ENGINE | Flat-6 1991 cc | Flat-6 2341 cc | Turbo flat-6 2994 cc |
| HORSEPOWER | 130 bhp @ 6100 rpm | 190 bhp @ 6500 rpm | 260 bhp @ 5500 rpm |
| TRANSMISSION | Manual 5-speed | Manual 5-speed | Manual 4-speed |
| CHASSIS | Unitary steel body/chassis with Targa-style option (*all models*) | | |
| BRAKES | Disc brakes all round (*all models*) | | |
| TOP SPEED | 130 mph | 147 mph | 155 mph |
| 0-60 MPH | 8.3 sec | 6.2 sec | 6.1 sec |
| 0-100 MPH | 24.3 sec | 17.1 sec | 14.5 sec |

*'This was a driver's car, and one that would keep going and going.'*

*Introduced in response to International racing rules, the 911 Turbo came in 1975; type-numbered 930, it was to sire the 934, 935 and 936 racing machinery.*

# PORSCHE 924, 944, 928

*'Like all Porsches they are classics in their own time.'*

Creating an entry level Porsche has always been difficult; if you make them in volume to get the price down you devalue the marque's exclusivity; and if you don't make them in volume you won't build them cheaply. Porsche twice tried to undertake a joint venture which would satisfy both sets of dealers, a cheaper car for Porsche, a sporting car for Volkswagen or Audi; but neither time did it work out as planned.

Porsche has always worked fairly closely with Volkswagen from the days of their common Beetle heritage. The Beetle and its off-spring were still going in the late 'sixties when Volkswagen wanted a sports car; the result was the mid-engined 914 which would be built by Karmann. Over the five years from 1970 some 120,000 of these VW-Porsches were built; Porsche preferred their own derivative, the 914/6 using the 911 engine, but that only lasted two years and neither car served the purpose as an entry level to the 911 world.

The VW-Audi group wanted Porsche to produce another sports car to follow the 914, although this would be an Audi, a more up-market name. Work started on the 924 as the 914 began production. It was to use a water-cooled 2-litre VW engine mounted in the front to allow 2+2 seating and reasonable luggage space. Part-way through the project, VW called a halt in 1974 in

the wake of the world energy crisis. The 914 was coming to an end, so Porsche took the plunge to buy out Audi's interest, which they achieved on the basis that the car would be built at the Audi-NSU plant in Neckarsulm – that suited Porsche as their own factory was full with renewed demand for the 911 and preparation for the new 928.

Work had started on the 928, the nominal 911 replacement, in 1971 with a view to phasing it in after 12 years or so of the 911's life. The new car would be be front-engined with a big V-8 to appeal to the American market and it would have two real seats in the back. Then came the 1973 Yom Kippur war and big V8s ceased to have appeal. The market looked brighter by 1975 but the 911 refused to die, so Porsche resolved to produce both, as well as the new 924. The chosen layout of the 928 – front engine and rear gearbox – influenced the final choice for the 924 transmission. The little car was launched in 1976 with the 928 following a year later, initially with a 4.5-litre engine developing 240 bhp.

The 924's single cam 2-litre engine produced 125 bhp and was good for around 125 mph with its low drag Porsche designed body. As ever, Porsche kept up a steady model development programme on the 924; a five-speed gearbox was standard by 1979, a 170 bhp 924 Turbo came in 1980 along with a 210 bhp Carrera GT competition version of the Turbo. That Carrera bodywork, a 924 shape with bulging wheel arch pods was exactly how the 944 would look when it arrived in 1982.

The 944 would be the next level, a 924 equipped with a genuine Porsche engine. The new 2.5-litre, canted over at 45 degrees, was a four-cylinder unit which used a certain amount of the thinking that went into the 928's V-8, with the added refinement of a pair of balancer shafts to smooth the natural vibrations of a big 'four'. The 944 had immediate appeal as a genuine Porsche, rather than an Audi-Porsche; even inserting the 944 engine into the 924S didn't give any great boost to the 924 range but it continued in production until 1988. The 944 had a turbo version in 1985 which raised the output to 217 bhp

*Initially an Audi joint development, the 924 used a 2-litre sohc VW engine with water cooling and front mounting being Porsche novelties. This 1978 car has had a competition career.*

and the top speed to over 150 mph. The 16-valve
944S followed in 1987, the same year that big
brother 928 appeared in 5-litre 32-valve form as
the S4 having had interim S and S2 models with
4.7-litre engines.

   The 944S went on to become the S2 with a 3-
litre engine developing 211 bhp and a lot more
torque, and then became the 968. The 928
meanwhile continues as the GTS and will soon be
clocking up its first 20 years. Like all Porsches they
are classics in their own time; even Porsche's
nominal joint ventures, the 914 and 924, have
classic status.

*Above right: For the 944, Porsche used their own 2.5-litre
'four' with twin balancer shafts, and wide-wheel body
restyling that had been used on the 924 Carrera GT.
Shown is a 1986 944.*

*Below: Porsche had planned the 928 as a 911 replacement, but
the 911 refused to die, so the four-seater 928 has continued
alongside from 1978 with a regular programme of
performance increases.*

| SPECIFICATION | 924<br>(1976) | 944<br>(1982) | 928<br>(1977) |
|---|---|---|---|
| ENGINE | 4-cyl 1984 cc | 4-cyl 2479 cc | V-8 4474 cc |
| HORSEPOWER | 125 bhp @ 5800 rpm | 163 bhp @ 5800 rpm | 240 bhp @ 5500 rpm |
| TRANSMISSION | Manual 4-speed | Manual 5-speed | Manual 5-speed |
| CHASSIS | Unitary steel with steel body panels (*all models*) | | |
| BRAKES | Disc/drum | All disc | All disc |
| TOP SPEED | 125 mph | 137 mph | 143 mph |
| 0-60 MPH<br>0-100 MPH | 10.1 sec<br>24.5 sec | 8.2 sec<br>20.9 sec | 7.4 sec<br>18.6 sec |

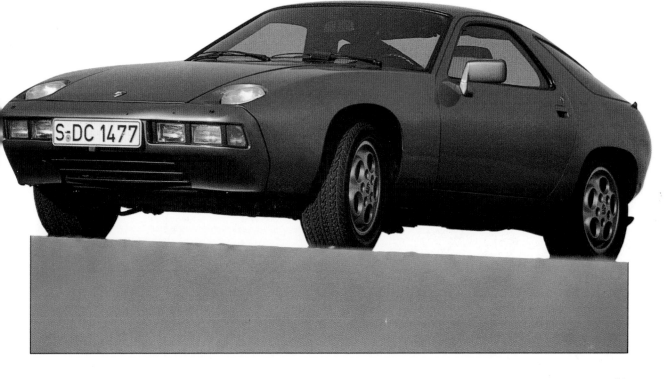

# STUDEBAKER COMMANDER, SILVER HAWK, AVANTI

*'Loewy coupés were world landmarks in modern elegant style.'*

Studebaker's origins date from its 1852 establishment as horse-drawn carriage makers. They switched to cars in 1902 but long-term commercial success was to elude them throughout their existence until car production ceased in 1965, but during that time they produced some remarkable cars, memorable particularly for the advanced styling of the post-war years, the products of Raymond Loewy, Studebaker's consultant from 1936.

In the 'twenties, they produced six and eight-cylinder engined cars, publicising them with long distance runs such as 30,000 miles in under 30,000 minutes in 1928; when Indianapolis accepted touring car engines, Studebaker engined cars took a 4th in 1931 and a 3rd in 1932. But despite the promotion, the Depression bit and the company went under in 1933. Revived, they were back in force by 1939 reaching 100,000 production with the $700 Champion as the mainstay.

After profitable war work Studebaker were out with striking-looking new models for 1947, the work of Virgil Exner at the Loewy studios; with

wings merged into the waistline they were well ahead of their time, particularly the Starlight Coupé with its four-piece wrap-round rear screen. The Champion used the pre-war 169 cu.in six and the bigger Commander a 226 cu.in (3.7-litre) version. For 1950 Loewy introduced the bullet-nose, a circular chromed intake flanked by head and sidelights arranged in a single vertical housing; in the same year the 1935-style transverse leaf independent front suspension was replaced by a coil spring system. Engineering kept up with style; a year later came the first overhead-valve V-8, a 232 cu.in. (3.8-litre) 120 bhp unit.

Striking though the previous models had been, the 1953 Loewy coupés were world landmarks in modern elegant style with minimal chromework, the best being the pillar-less Starliner; the four-door saloons were still striking but not as dramatic. Engines were the old Champion 'six' now at 185 cu.in and the 120 bhp V-8. These models continued with minor changes until 1956, to be replaced by the Hawks.

Low and sporting, these too were styled by

In an age when fins and chrome were infecting style, the Loewy-designed Commander was elegantly restrained; this is a 1954 model.

*Loewy's final fling for Studebaker produced the legendary Avanti for 1962 with the coke-bottle styling for its glass-fibre bodywork. It failed to save the company but lived on through other owners.*

Loewy; while the centre section was little changed, the rear began to grow fins and the front took on a more conventional grille shape. The range included the Power Hawk using a 4.7-litre version of the V-8 and the top Golden Hawk powered by a 5.8-litre Packard engine – Packard had been taken over by Studebaker but was to die by 1958. For 1957, the Packard unit was replaced by a supercharged version of the Studebaker 4.7-litre 289 and the Silver Hawk adopted the normal unit. In an age of excess, the Hawks' comparative restraint stood out – they were almost as impressive as the 1953 cars had been.

Interesting though the Studebaker models were, they were fighting a losing battle against the big three engaged in their own price-cutting wars – good for the consumer but bad for the smaller rivals; being based in Indiana, away from the mainstream suppliers didn't help. The company went for volume by leading into the Compact market – the 1959 Lark, a shortened saloon, was an immediate success in modest Studebaker terms and gave them some breathing space.

They now needed a new sports coupé and once more turned to Raymond Loewy, who came up with the fascinating Avanti for 1962; its exceptionally clean lines included a grille-less front with the air intake beneath the bumper, and the start of the renowned 'Coke-bottle' waist-line. With glass-fibre bodywork it had a steel chassis to carry the familiar 4.7-litre V-8 with supercharged options giving 240 and 290 bhp; it was also the first American chassis to carry front disc brakes as standard. Fewer than 4500 had been built by the time that Studebaker production ceased at Indiana in early 1964; although Larks continued to be

made in Canada using Chevrolet engines until 1966, the Avanti was left behind. Its production was taken over by two South Bend dealers in 1965; using Chevrolet power, it was to continue in limited numbers until 1991, by which time it had new owners in Ohio. Along the way, a convertible and a four-door version were added. Even now, it is a striking looking car, the final tribute to the Loewy designs for Studebaker.

*Arriving in 1956, the Hawks were recognisably evolutions of the Commander series with restrained period fins and a more normal grille shape; the powerful Golden Hawk was top of a range which included Power Hawk and Silver Hawk, 1958 version shown here.*

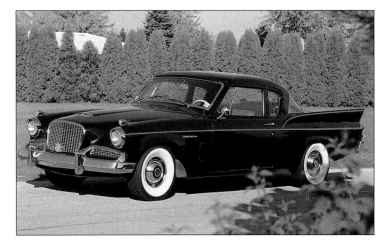

| SPECIFICATION | COMMANDER (1953) | SILVER HAWK (1961) | AVANTI (1963) |
|---|---|---|---|
| ENGINE | Iron V-8, 3813 cc | Iron V-8, 4735 cc | S/c V-8, 4735 cc |
| POWER | 120 bhp @ 4000 rpm | 210 bhp @ 4500 rpm | 290 bhp @ 5200 rpm |
| TRANSMISSION | Manual 3-speed | Manual 4-speed | Manual 4-speed |
| CHASSIS | Steel frame | Steel frame | Steel, grp body |
| BRAKES | Drums | Drums | Disc/drum |
| TOP SPEED | 95 mph | 115 mph | 125 mph |
| 0-60 MPH | 14.9 sec | 10.2 sec | 8.8 sec |

# SUNBEAM TALBOT ALPINE, ALPINE MK.II, TIGER

*'It was attractive although the rear fins were too pronounced for some tastes.'*

The louvred bonnet and the long sloping tail gave the 1953-5 Alpine a very sporting appearance which was backed by rally successes.

The Rootes Group had been assembled in the 'thirties with the merger of Humber and Hillman followed by the 1935 acquisitions of Sunbeam and Talbot. Despite their individual illustrious past histories, neither of the latter marques contributed to Rootes' design – they were just names to be used in badge engineering of the solid, dependable Hillman and Humber ranges. While there was initially a Talbot Ten, the Sunbeam name lay fallow until the 1938 arrival of a Sunbeam-Talbot range – double-barrelled names suggested class at the time – with a Ten and two short-lived six-cylinder cars, joined by a 2-litre as war broke out.

While the Ten and 2-litre were renewed after the war, both were replaced by the 80 and 90 in 1948. These used overhead valve versions of pre-war 1185 cc Minx and 1944 cc Hawk engines in pre-war beam-axled chassis, with their own attractive saloon and convertible models. The 80 didn't reach Mk.II form, but the 90 Mk.II came in 1950 with an all-new, but still separate, chassis with independent front suspension, and an engine increased to 2267 cc with 70 bhp. This model soon clocked up rally successes and formed the basis of the long-standing Rootes competition department; rally work led to the Mk.IIA in 1952 with bigger brakes, 77 bhp and a maximum speed around 82 mph. And it was rally success that led to the 1953 launch of a sporting two-seater version of the Mk.IIA – the Alpine; as this was essentially for export to the USA where Talbot meant little, it was marketed there as the Sunbeam Alpine although Sunbeam-Talbot was to remain the marque name in Europe for another year. The chassis was stiffened to compensate for the loss of the roof and the engine output was increased to 80 bhp which gave the sleek new model 95 mph performance. By then, though, Healeys and Triumphs were faster and cheaper, so the first Alpine died after just two years in 1955; the IIA's successor, the Sunbeam Mk.III continued from 1954 to 1957, taking advantage of the Alpine's 80 bhp engine.

Meanwhile the Rootes Group had launched a new range of unitary construction family saloons in 1955 with the Hillman Minx, Singer Gazelle and Sunbeam Rapier supplemented by the Husky van which used the same platform with 10 inches removed from the wheelbase. Initially the saloons had 1390 cc ohv engines, rising to 1494 cc in 1958; for the Rapier Mk.II this gave 68 bhp. For 1959 the Alpine name returned for a new two-seater built up on the Husky platform with uprated Rapier running gear including an aluminium head, disc front brakes and 13-inch wheels. With in-house styling once more mainly for the American market, it was attractive although the rear fins were too pronounced for some tastes. With 78 bhp, it wasn't quite a 100 mph car, and the extra 2 bhp from the 1594 cc Mk.II a year later made little difference.

Chassis improvements and a choice of GT (with detachable hard-top) or the more powerful 82 bhp Tourer denoted the Mk.III's arrival in 1960. The hard-top was square-rigged and spacious and justified the creation of small +2 seating. It was less than a year later that the Mk.IV arrived with its fins cut back to the vertical to make a much better balanced shape; an auto-box option was offered for the first time. After some 50,000 units of the 4 models in six years, the final Alpine Mk.V came in 1965 using the 1725 cc engine with 92.5 bhp; by the time the model was phased out in 1968, a total of nearly 70,000 had been built. The Alpines were always more comfortably trimmed and arguably better built than the rival MGs and TRs, but were never genuine 100 mph cars.

For those that liked the Alpine's style and comfort but also wanted genuine high performance, there was the sadly short-lived Tiger based on the

Series IV. Taking a leaf from the AC Cobra story, the same 4.2-litre (260 cu.in) Ford V-8 was successfully inserted by an American dealer and became a production reality in 1964. American gearbox, stronger back axle with Panhard rod location, and rack and pinion steering contributed to the Alpine's ability to accept a 137% increase in torque, while the 75% power increase brought the top speed to nearly 120 mph. Nearly 6500 were produced in two years before a mere 571 Tiger IIs were built with the 4.7-litre Ford V-8 in 1967. Meanwhile Chrysler had become shareholders in 1964 and taken over in 1967 — the Ford-powered Tiger was an inevitable casualty.

Right: The second generation Alpines were based on the Hillman Husky van chassis, using the period best of the ohv 'four' range. Despite sports car looks they were never 100mph cars. This is a 1966 Alpine Mk.V — with detachable hardtop.

Below: Putting the 4.2 litre Ford V-8 into a strengthened Alpine Series IV gave instant high performance and a strong basis for a successful rally car, this being an ex-works 1964 team car.

| SPECIFICATION | ALPINE (1954) | ALPINE SERIES (1960) | TIGER (1965) |
|---|---|---|---|
| ENGINE | 4-cyl, 2267 cc | 4-cyl,1594 cc | V-8,4261 cc |
| POWER | 80 bhp @ 4200 rpm | 80 bhp @ 5000 rpm | 141 bhp @ 4400 rpm |
| TRANSMISSION | Manual 4-speed | Manual 4-speed + o/d | Manual 4-speed |
| CHASSIS | Steel frame and body | Unitary steel | Unitary steel |
| BRAKES | Drums | Disc/drum | Disc/drum |
| TOP SPEED | 95 mph | 99mph | 116 mph |
| 0-60 MPH<br>0-100 MPH | 18.9 sec<br>— | 13.6 sec<br>— | 9.4 sec<br>30.6 sec |

# TOYOTA 2000GT, CELICA, MR2

*'The MR2 would give 120 mph performance and superb roadholdling in a neatly styled sporting package.'*

Toyota was relatively late on the automotive scene. Although the Toyoda Automatic Loom works was founded in 1926, and an automobile section was set up in 1933, the plant wasn't completed until 1937 and few cars had been produced by the outbreak of war. Car production resumed in 1949; where other Japanese companies had initially built foreign cars under licence, Toyota developed their own range of saloons initially for the home market but with an eye to export. By the end of the 'fifties, production had gradually built up to 30,000 cars a year but was to accelerate rapidly from then. By 1965, it had reached 230,000 cars a year of which 20% were exported. As all these were family saloons, the announcement of such an overtly sporting coupé as the Toyota 2000GT was something of a surprise.

In fact, the 2000GT started life as the Goertz-styled car that Nissan sub-contracted Yamaha to produce in 1963. Yamaha Motor Company had been separately founded in 1955 to major on motor-cycles but to develop a general transport engineering ability, including the production of sporting engines for other manufacturers. Nissan didn't take up the project once the prototype was completed, so it was offered to Toyota with whom it was then co-developed; the 2000GT was launched at the 1965 Tokyo Motor Show but it was to be another two years before the car went

*With E-type looks and a twin-cam engine Toyota's first sports car was right up-to-date when first shown in 1965; although too expensive, it was a strong pointer to the future.*

into limited production at Yamaha's Yamamatsu Headquarters.

The design was very much European influenced. While Toyota's own cars were using a separate cruciform frame, the 2000GT copied the Lotus sheet steel backbone system, but then used a steel bodyshell to increase the torsional stiffness. Suspension front and rear used double wishbones and coil springs with rack and pinion steering, while Dunlop disc brakes were made under licence by Sumitomo. Using the Crown's 2-litre seven-bearing six-cylinder as a basis, Yamaha designed an aluminium twin-cam head to develop 150 bhp at 6600 rpm, while an extra gear was grafted onto the back of the Crown's four-speed box. With an E-type style two-seater coupé body, it was an attractive car and concept. During 1966, a lightweight version had won the Suzuka 1000 Km race and taken a number of International records in a 72-hour endurance run. It should have been a success, particularly in America, but only 351 were produced – virtually hand-made, they were too expensive to build and couldn't justify a higher price than the Jaguar. If it didn't work for Toyota, it did for Yamaha – they still build most of Toyota's multi-valve engines.

While Toyota produced two-door coupé models within most of their saloon ranges in the late 'sixties, it wasn't until 1970 that a sporting version received its own model name; the two door

*The second generation Celica came in 1977 including this neat 2000ST coupé.*

Celica and the four-door Carina were developments of the previous Corona and shared the same chassis, but different body panels created entirely different styles. A neat 4-seater coupé with European appeal, the Celica was powered by a cross-flow 1600 cc 'four' with 105 bhp, enough to reach 104 mph; while its details showed a period Japanese fussiness with a nondescript full-width grille, the style showed promise. In competition trim, it made its mark in rallies while the twin-cam engine became the top F3 power unit. The 1977 replacements included a lift-back coupé with a choice of 2-litre engines including the twin-cam 2000GT with 118 bhp. The third generation came in 1981 with all-independent suspension and some 4-valve engines, with the front-drive fourth generation arriving in 1985. In ever more sophisticated forms the Celica is still with us and has been one of Toyota's best exports. Meanwhile a six-cylinder version had been added in 1981 as the Celica Supra, but this became a model name in its own right for 1985; it is still their supercar flagship.

Meanwhile Toyota's sporting successes had led to the introduction of the mid-engined MR2 in 1984; taking a leaf from the Fiat X1/9 book, it used a transverse front-drive power pack from the Corolla and set it amidships. With the 16-valve 120 bhp 'four', the MR2 would give 120 mph performance and superb roadholding in a neatly styled sporting package. A T-bar version – twin removable roof-halves – came in 1987; the first generation was phased out in 1990 to be replaced by faster models with even better roadholding. Despite a shaky sports car start with the 2000GT, Toyota's sporting machinery is now among the world's best.

*Below: Arriving in 1984, the MR2 followed the simple formula of the Fiat X1/9 with a front-wheel-drive package reversed behind the cockpit. A T-bar roof came in 1987.*

| SPECIFICATION | 2000GT (1967) | CELICA 1.6 (1971) | MR2 (1986) |
|---|---|---|---|
| ENGINE | Dohc 6-cyl, 1988 cc | Four-cyl, 1558 cc | Dohc 4-cyl, 1587 cc |
| POWER | 150 bhp @ 6600 rpm | 105 bhp @ 6000 rpm | 135 bhp @ 6600 rpm |
| TRANSMISSION | Manual 5-speed | Manual 4-speed | Manual 5-speed |
| CHASSIS | Steel frame and body | Unitary steel | Unitary steel |
| BRAKES | Discs | Disc/drum | Discs |
| TOP SPEED | 132 mph | 104 mph | 122 mph |
| 0-60 MPH 0-100 MPH | 9.8 sec 24.8 sec | 11.5 sec — | 8.0 sec 21.6 sec |

# TRIUMPH TR2, TR4, TR6

*'Originally a motor-cycle company, Triumph began to produce small cars from 1923.'*

Launched in definitive form at Geneva in March 1953, the TR2 was the best value 100 mph sports car and soon established the Triumph name in sporting circles. This 1954 TR2 has a later TR3A grille.

Now just another vanished name, Triumph, along with MG and Austin-Healey, was one of the star players in the economy sports car market that was such a British preserve through the 'fifties and 'sixties.

Originally a motor-cycle company, Triumph began to produce small cars from 1923; moving up-market for the 'thirties gave more prestige but the investment required for a new range of engines was to bring the company down before the outbreak of war; the motor-cycle business was another casualty, having been sold off in 1936. However some rally successes had been achieved in the hands of the Technical Director Donald Healey. Meanwhile Standard had been building sensible family cars for many years and had also supplied the pre-war SS Cars with chassis and engines; they at least had a feel for sports cars but no reputation. Standard thus absorbed the Triumph name, all that was left, in the latter part of the war to use as the up-market and sporting Standard, when post-war design could resume.

The first sporting Triumph came in 1946; the 1800 Roadster was built up on the pre-war Standard 14 chassis but it lacked the speed and style to be a real sports car. It was fortunate that Standard-Triumph's Sir John Black did a deal with tractor magnate Harry Ferguson to build tractors for him around a new power unit which could double as tractor and car power; modelled on the pre-war Citroen unit, this was the big ohv 'four' designed with wet liner cylinders for easy repair and simple capacity adjustment. While the new engine went into the hump-backed Standard Vanguard and the Triumph Roadster 2000 in 1948, Sir John Black still wanted a real sports car – preferably to sell at £500 – for the export market.

After two false starts, the definitive Triumph TR2 arrived at the Geneva Motor Show in March 1953; a short-tailed prototype had been seen at Earls Court in October 1952, but a lot of development work had gone on in between, including an increase in power for the 2-litre engine from 75 bhp to 90 bhp – enough for an easy 100 mph car. The TR2 had its own separate chassis frame but used front suspension and rear axle from the Mayflower saloon while its neat and modern body had been designed by Walter Belgrove, who had drawn up the pre-war Triumphs. Its pre-tax UK price was £555 against

*The TR6 proved a best-seller – this is a 1972 model.*

the MG TF at £550 or the Austin-Healey 100 at £750 while the XK120 started at £1130; it was a good value performance package but production was slow to get under way. Only some 8600 TR2s had been built by the time the TR3 arrived in October 1955, but 30 per cent, remained in the United Kingdom.

The TR3 showed little change – an egg-box grille in the intake, sliding panel side-screens, and bigger carburetters to take the power up to 95 bhp – but it was to be produced in much greater numbers. Power rose to 100 bhp the following year and disc front brakes became standard at the end of 1956. A year later came the TR3A with a full-width grille with other detail changes.

With the help of Italian stylist Michelotti, the new-shaped TR4 arrived in September 1961; wind-up windows, an optional Surrey hard-top, face-level ventilation, and considerably more space made this a very civilised car. Under the skin the engine had been enlarged to 2138 cc while rack and pinion steering was fitted to a wider chassis. TR enthusiasts had to wait until March 1965 before criticism of the hard ride was countered with the TR4A and its all-new chassis with independent rear suspension.

Meanwhile the 4-cylinder engine was getting a little too old and unsuited to emission laws. Announced in late 1967, the bodily unchanged TR5 used a 2.5-litre version of the Triumph 6-cylinder engine in 142 bhp fuel-injection form, or for America as the TR250 with carburetters and a mere 104 bhp. This only had a brief run before the

TR6 arrived in January 1969; front and rear panels revised by Karmann transformed its looks although there were few other changes. This final separate-chassis TR6 was actually the most popular TR with 91,850 models produced during its 8-year spell as part of a total of over a quarter-million real TRs - TR2 to TR6.

*Below: While TR3, TR3A and TR4 followed the TR2 design with revised bodywork and a steady increase in power, it was not until 1965 that the TR4A came out with independent rear suspension.*

| SPECIFICATION | TR2 (1954) | TR4 (1962) | TR6 (1969) |
|---|---|---|---|
| ENGINE | 4-cyl, 1991 cc | 4-cyl, 2138 cc | 6-cyl, 2498 cc |
| POWER | 90 bhp @ 4800 rpm | 100 bhp @ 4600 rpm | 142 bhp @ 5500 rpm |
| TRANSMISSION | Manual 4-speed + optional overdrive (all models) | | |
| CHASSIS | Separate steel frame chassis with steel body panels (all models) | | |
| BRAKES | Drums | Disc/drum | Disc/drum |
| TOP SPEED | 107 mph | 109 mph | 117 mph |
| 0-60 MPH 0-100 MPH | 12.0 sec — | 10.9 sec 39.9 sec | 8.5 sec 24.7 sec |

# TVR GRANTURA MK.II, TAIMAR, TASMIN

*'All models have been pretty exclusive and arguably classics in their own time.'*

For over 40 years now the unlikely venue of Blackpool has played host to the charismatic TVR. The company is the only one of the rash of 'fifties special-builders to have survived, although it too has had its share of ups and downs, receiverships and ownership changes. But throughout it all, the TVR has remained an enthusiast's car, right for the period; perhaps the early ones were not such good value in performance terms as in exclusivity, but for the last twenty years a TVR has been a fast car.

The basic principles of the TVR have remained unchanged. The chassis has always been a built up tubular frame which has become even stiffer over the years; the original Grantura Mk.I and II used the independent front suspension of a VW Beetle at both ends but from the 1962 Mk.III onwards full wishbone systems have been used, usually made by TVR but attached to a proprietary upright. The chassis was lengthened from the original overly short 7ft wheelbase to 7ft.6in many years back and the cars have always been two-seaters until the arrival of the current Cerbera. Fortunately there has been no reluctance

to supply engines even from a major to a minor in the same market; TVR have used Coventry Climax, MG, Triumph, Ford's 4-cyl, V-6 and American V-8 engines, with modified Rover power most popular from the mid-'eighties.

Bodies have always been built within TVR in high-quality glassfibre. The original rounded dumpy look of the first 1958 cars gave way to the Manx tail in 1964. The similar but longer M-series body came on a new stiffer chassis in 1972. The hatchback Taimar came in 1976 and the Convertible in 1978, both using Ford V-6 3-litre power. New for the 'eighties was the sleeker, sharper Tasmin shape with a 7ft.10 in wheelbase which was to come in lift-back, 2+ (very little) 2 and convertible forms. Initially the engine was the German Ford V-6 2.8-litre, but the Pinto 2-litre was available from 1981; then 1983 saw the 3.5-litre Rover at which point the Tasmin name was dropped in favour of engine-related numbers.

By this time TVR prices had moved steadily upmarket and were looking overly expensive; the cars were always very well finished, with comfortable leather interiors, and took many hours to build with a lot of parts bought from outside. The 1986 Convertible S was a much simplified car modelled on the original convertible and, with the

*While this Grantura Mk.III is virtually identical to the Mk.II, the chassis was all new and featured wishbone suspension instead of the VW-based trailing arms.*

Ford V-6, was 25% cheaper; for 1988, 515 of the 701 cars produced were the S model. This paved the way for the new Griffith 4.3 in 1992 – sophisticated high performance in a nostalgic package.

TVR have never quite reached the 20 cars per week level, so all models have been pretty exclusive and arguably classics in their own time; until the current series, no single model has had 1000 examples. So what to feature, apart from one per decade? The cars that set TVR on the map were the original short-wheelbase VW-suspended Mk.II Granturas; around 400 were produced of which the MGA 1600 engined cars were the most popular and indeed formed the basis of TVR's attempts at International racing at the time. Being some 350 lb lighter than the MGA, the TVR was faster off the mark and would reach 60 mph in 12.0 sec against the MG's 13.3 sec – it was also 2 mph faster; but at £1184 inc taxes in 1961 it was also £157 more expensive than the MGA coupé, reflecting a small price for exclusivity.

While the Triumph-engined 2500M from 1972-77 was the most popular of that series, the majority of the 947 built went to America. The 3000M, with Ford V-6 power, was better known in Europe and was the basis for the Taimar/Convertible/Turbo models; there were 1370 variations on the 3000M theme of which 63 were the Broadspeed Turbos with 230 bhp rather than 140 bhp. The hatch-back Taimar was a truly practical TVR.

From the 'eighties, one can only choose a Tasmin shape. While the Ford V-6 2.8-litre was the mainstay in the first half of the 'eighties, the first of the Rover V-8 powered cars is the more significant – the 350i. The Tasmins were some 300 lb heavier than the preceding 3000M series, so needed the extra power to stay ahead. Both, however, had four-cylinder equivalents for those less interested in sporting acceleration. TVRs could be all things to all people.

*Above: After years of evolution, the 1980 Tasmin was the start of a new style. This early model was powered by the German Ford V-6. By 1983, the Rover V-8 had been adopted for the 350i.*

*The hatch-back Taimar used the 3-litre Ford V-6 to give a practical 120 mph 2-seater sports coupé.*

| SPECIFICATION | GRANTURA Mk.II (1961) | 3000M (1974) | 350i (1984) |
|---|---|---|---|
| ENGINE | MG 4-cyl, 1588 cc | Ford V-6, 2994 cc | Rover V-8, 3528 cc |
| POWER | 79 bhp @ 5600 rpm | 138 bhp @ 5000 rpm | 197 bhp @ 5300 rpm |
| TRANSMISSION | Manual 4-speed | Manual 4-speed | Manual 5-speed |
| CHASSIS | Tubular steel chassis, all-independent suspension, glassfibre bodywork | | |
| BRAKES | Disc/drum | Disc/drum | Discs |
| TOP SPEED | 98 mph | 121 mph | 136 mph |
| 0-60 MPH  0-100 MPH | 12.0 sec  — | 7.7 sec  25.6 sec | 6.6 sec  20.2 sec |

# CHIC SALOONS – VW BEETLE, CITROEN 2CV, MORRIS MINOR

*Opposite: This 1970 Beetle may have changed somewhat in detail, but the design is still that of Professor Porsche's pre-war Peoples' Car; more Beetles have been built than any other car.*

*Built to carry the goods and chattels of the French agricultural worker, the Deux Chevaux provided cheap and entertaining, if slow, motoring for many more.*

Classics don't have to be sporting cars to be appreciated, although it helps. There are, though, a handful of mass-production small saloons that became cult cars during their own lifetimes; they fulfilled the market need but they did it differently whether through particularly clever engineering or quirky styling, or a mixture of the two, and demand was such that production went on and on. Cult status breeds longevity which increases the cult status.

Our chosen trio all started production shortly after the war, although the designs had been under way for some time. First away was the Volkswagen designed by Professor Porsche in response to Hitler's demand for a people's car shortly after he became Chancellor in 1933; the contract was signed in June 1934 and the first car was shown in February 1936. After three sets of prototypes the final version evolved with a view to production starting at Wolfsburg in mid-1939 but war stopped that. Design novelties included the all-independent suspension whose torsion bar trailing arm and swing axle systems had been seen on the Auto Union GP car, and the air-cooled flat four engine mounted behind the rear axle; these were mounted within a platform chassis under the beetle-shaped skin that was to remain throughout a life that extends to the present day – swing axle Beetles are

still made in Mexico with 44 bhp 1600 cc engines. Beetle production started slowly in 1945 with 1131 cc and a 65 mph maximum. Exports began in 1949. Over the years the engine was steadily enlarged through 1200, 1300 and 1500 cc while the body and windows had detail changes; the first design change came in 1970 with the 1302 when MacPherson struts and semi-trailing arm suspension made the handing considerably less wayward. By 1973 the Beetle had passed the American Model T Ford record of 16.5 million and ensured its place in history.

Production of the 2CV from 1948-90 passed the 5-million mark but this was mostly confined to mainland Europe; it was never going to appeal to the US in any numbers. Design work started on this in 1936 using much the same team as had created the Light Fifteen, hence the front-wheel-drive; work was still under way at the outbreak of war and continued during it, although little was to change by the time the car was finally launched in 1948. It was intended to be totally reliable whatever the treatment it received from first-time motorists – like the Ford Model T. The air-cooled flat-twin engine was only 375 cc and developed all of 9 bhp which was enough to give a maximum of 40 mph. Interconnected front leading/rear trailing arm independent suspension with long wheel travel gave a remarkable ride that would allow easy carriage of eggs or people. Bodywork was extremely simple, thus repairable; the canvas roof would fold all the way back to provide fresh air and extra carrying capacity. It was odd in the extreme but very effective. In 1954 the engine was increased to 425 cc and 12 bhp which allowed 50 mph and in 1971 a 602 cc 26 bhp version was available as the 2CV6 – the new engine having come from the more upmarket Dyane.

Demand for the 2CV had picked up in the aftermath of the 1973 fuel crisis, but dwindled thereafter – it was, however, well established by then as a quirky classic.

Like the others, the Minor was conceived as a

universal people carrier but production only ever reached 1.2-million during its 1948-71 span. Much of it was fairly straightforward — a unitary platform chassis, leaf-sprung live rear axle, 918 cc side-valve engine from the pre-war Morris 8; but torsion bar front suspension with rack and pinion steering gave it remarkably sporting roadholding. Its styling was scaled-down American and it seated four in comfort — an extra four inches was added to its width at quite a late stage of development. Its appeal was based on a mixture of looks, small-car comfort and its sporting performance, whether in its 'woodie' Traveller, convertible or saloon forms. When BMC was formed in 1952, the side-valve engine was replaced by Austin's A-series and the Minor used most of its capacity variations over the years — 803, 948, 1098 cc — while maximum speed went up from 60 mph to nearly 80 mph.

The Minor might have been replaced by what became the Riley 1.5/Wolseley 1500 in the late 'fifties, but the market wouldn't allow it to die; eventually it was replaced in 1971 by the unloved Marina. But it still stands out as a very good simple family four seater.

*Inset below: Universal UK motoring was provided by the Minor which combined style with sporting handling. This 1948 version has the split windscreen and low headlights that distinguished the early cars.*

| SPECIFICATION | VW 'BEETLE' (1952) | CITROEN 2CV (1950) | MORRIS MINOR (1948) |
|---|---|---|---|
| ENGINE | Flat-4, 1131 cc | Flat-twin, 375 cc | 4-cyl, 918 cc |
| POWER | 25 bhp @ 3300 rpm | 9 bhp @ 3500 rpm | 28 bhp @ 4400 rpm |
| TRANSMISSION | Manual 4-speed | Manual 4-speed | Manual 4-speed |
| CHASSIS | Steel platform | Unitary platform | Unitary steel |
| BRAKES | Drums | Drums | Drums |
| TOP SPEED | 64 mph | 41mph | 62 mph |
| 0-30 MPH | 8.3 sec | 10.6 sec | 9.7 sec |
| 0-50 MPH | 22.1 sec | — | 32.5 sec |

# SUPERCARS – PORSCHE 959, JAGUAR XJ220, MCLAREN F1

*'The 959 was the ultimate Porsche 911 with its twin-turbocharged 450 bhp engine.'*

It is a long-trumpeted theme that motor sport improves the breed, the arrival of disc brakes being the most oft-cited example. But sometimes motor sport creates a new breed and few more exciting road cars have emerged than during the short-lived period of International Group B competition following a 1982 rule change.

International motor sport has always been largely based on developed road cars, although the outright racing cars have received greater promotion. Rules define the limits to which all must work, but the Group B rules just said that 200 must have been built within 12 months and laid down a few road car dimensions; the number is just big enough to ensure that the factory has to sell a reasonable number to the general public. The rally world responded with a mixture of purpose-built devices like the Ford RS200, purpose-built under a production shape – Metro 6R4 – and highly developed road cars like the Lancia Delta Integrale and Audis. There was also the Porsche 959 which was created for general Group B use, whether for race-track or the long-distance rally-raids.

The 959 was the ultimate Porsche 911 with its twin-turbocharged 450 bhp engine, electronically controlled four-wheel drive and composite body panels. It was first shown as a design study in 1981, getting into production in 1985 after further work; the 200 were not completed until 1986 at which point the rally rules changed to exclude the very

fast specials although rally raids continued to accept them. In the end 250 959s were built; some ten years on, the latest Turbo embodies much of the same competition-proved technology.

While the 959 was the first of the new breed of 200 mph supercar to be shown, the Ferrari 288GTO was the first to get into production. Obviously not a rally car, the new GTO was based on the assumption that Group B racing would become a serious category; while there were group B classes, such events were dominated by the sports-racing Group C cars, so the 288GTO never took to the tracks, but some 260 were built. With this car, Ferrari had set a trend by taking large deposits against later delivery when the first car was shown at Geneva in 1984; Aston Martin did the same the following year with the Vantage Zagato – it wasn't a racer, so was made even more exclusive with just 50 to be built.

With deposits and premium prices everyone wanted to get into the supercar act; it seemed that whatever was available, fast and exclusive would be bought, whether by real enthusiasts or premium-price speculators. Jaguar's XJ220 was the next to be unveiled at the 1988 Motor Show as a technical wonder based on the recent V-12 Le Mans cars with the addition of four-wheel-drive; Jaguar couldn't produce it within their own system so it was given to JaguarSport to develop. They removed the four-wheel-drive and substituted the later racing 3.5-litre V-6 turbo for the traditional

*Long, low and wide, the XJ220 is a big car in any company. While the original show car had a V-12 and 4WD, the production car used a turbo V-6 and 2WD to keep the size and weight down.*

The McLaren F1 will probably remain the fastest ever production car – and the most expensive too.

V-12; it was still very fast but not exactly what every Jaguar enthusiast had been expecting. And it hit the downside of the 'eighties boom, so only 280 of the planned 350 were built .

While Lamborghini continued to produce their own brand of regular supercar – Countach followed by Diablo – another four-wheel-drive multi-turbo 3.5-litre race-technology device was being launched just down the road; the 200 mph Bugatti EB110 was first shown in September 1991. This is still in slow production.

Last of the 200 mph club to be revealed was the McLaren F1 which was launched at Monaco in May 1992, some 4 years after the project got under way. This too is full of race-technology with carbon fibre composites used extensively in chassis and body. Its 6.1-litre BMW V-12 produces a remarkable 627 bhp and the car is electrifyingly fast, faster than anything else sold for the road. And it carries racing design through to the central driving position; the driver sits ahead of two passengers who are staggered slightly behind. It is the ultimate *Grand Prix* car for the road; the plan was to build 350 over 7 years. Time will tell how many, but meanwhile the F1 has gained an extra dimension.

Group B racing had inspired the arrival of the Porsche 959 and Ferrari 288GTO, and then let them down. But now a similar formula has returned as the leading sports car series. The McLaren is currently one of the best suited for this and victory in the 1995 Le Mans 24-hour race can only increase its appeal.

Below: Recognisably Porsche 911 in parts, the 959 used many composite body panels.

| SPECIFICATION | PORSCHE 959 (1988) | JAGUAR XJ220 (1993) | McLAREN F1 (1994) |
|---|---|---|---|
| ENGINE | Flat-6 turbo 2850 cc | V-6 turbo, 3498 cc | V-12, 6064 cc |
| POWER | 450 bhp at 6500 rpm | 549 bhp @ 7000 rpm | 627 bhp @ 7400 rpm |
| TRANSMISSION | Manual 6-speed 4WD | Manual 5-speed | Manual 6-speed |
| CHASSIS | Steel and Kevlar | Ali composite | C/fibre composite |
| BRAKES | Discs with ABS | Discs all round | Discs all round |
| MAXIMUM SPEED | 197 mph | 217 mph | 231 mph |
| 0-60 MPH 0-100 MPH | 3.7 sec 8.5 sec | 3.6 sec 7.9 sec | 3.2 sec 6.3 sec |

CARS

# INDEX

NB Cars listed in Contents are not included here.

Appleyard, Ian . . . . . . . . . . . . . . . . . . . . . . . . 46
Arkus-Duntov, Zora . . . . . . . . . . . . . . . . . . . 26
Armstrong-Siddeley . . . . . . . . . . . . . . . . . . . 46
Austin 7 . . . . . . . . . . . . . . . . . . . . . . . . . . . . . 22

Belgrove, Walter . . . . . . . . . . . . . . . . . . . . . . 88
Bertone, Carrozzeria . . 10, 12, 16, 32, 52, 54, 56
Bizzarrini, Giotto . . . . . . . . . . . . . . . . . . . . . 52
Black, Sir John . . . . . . . . . . . . . . . . . . . . . . . 88
Blatchley, John . . . . . . . . . . . . . . . . . . . . . . . 20
BMW 328 . . . . . . . . . . . . . . . . . . . . . . . . . . . . 8
Bristol . . . . . . . . . . . . . . . . . . . . . . . . 8, 22, 28
Bugatti EB110 . . . . . . . . . . . . . . . . . . . . . . . . 94

Chapman, Colin . . . . . . . . . . . . . . . . . . . 58, 60
Cisitalia GT . . . . . . . . . . . . . . . . . . . . . . 20, 56
Coaker, Gerry . . . . . . . . . . . . . . . . . . . . . . . . 18
Cole, Ed . . . . . . . . . . . . . . . . . . . . . . . . . . . . 24
Colombo, Gioacchino . . . . . . . . . . . . . . . . . . 34
Costin, Frank . . . . . . . . . . . . . . . . . . . . . . . . 58
Coventry-Climax . . . . . . . . . . . . . . . . . . 58, 70

Dallara, Giampaolo . . . . . . . . . . . . . . . . 52, 54
Dixi . . . . . . . . . . . . . . . . . . . . . . . . . . . . . . . . 22

Earl, Harley . . . . . . . . . . . . . . . . . . . . . . . . . 26
Enever, Syd . . . . . . . . . . . . . . . . . . . . . . . . . . 68
Evernden, Ivan . . . . . . . . . . . . . . . . . . . . . . . 20
Exner, Virgil . . . . . . . . . . . . . . . . . . . . . . 28, 82
Facel Vega . . . . . . . . . . . . . . . . . . . . . . . . . . . 28
Ferguson, Harry . . . . . . . . . . . . . . . . . . . . . . 88
Fiat X1/9 . . . . . . . . . . . . . . . . . . . . 56, 74, 86
Frazer Nash . . . . . . . . . . . . . . . . . . . . . . . . . 18
Frua, Carrozzeria . . . . . . . . . . . . . . . . . . . . . 62

Gandini, Marcello . . . . . . . . . . . . . . . . . . . . 54
Ghia, Carrozzeria . . . . . . . . . . . . . . . . . . . . . 28
Giugiaro/ItalDesign . . . . . . . . . . . . . . . . 60, 62
Goertz, Albrecht . . . . . . . . . . . . . . . . . . . 72, 86
Greenley, Ken . . . . . . . . . . . . . . . . . . . . . . . . 20

Healey, Donald . . . . . . . . . . . . . . . . . . . 18, 88
Heffernan, John . . . . . . . . . . . . . . . . . . . . . . 20
H.J.Mulliner . . . . . . . . . . . . . . . . . . . . . . . . . 20
Hoffman, Max . . . . . . . . . . . . . . . . . . . . . . . . 64

Iacocca, 'Lee' . . . . . . . . . . . . . . . . . . . . . . . . 44
Isetta, BMW . . . . . . . . . . . . . . . . . . . . . . . . . 22
Iso Rivolta . . . . . . . . . . . . . . . . . . . . . . . . . . . 52

Jano, Vittorio . . . . . . . . . . . . . . . . . . . . . 32, 56
Jensen Motors . . . . . . . . . . . . . . . . . 18, 28, 60

Karmann, Karosserie . . . . . . . . . . . . . . . . . . 88
Kimber, Cecil . . . . . . . . . . . . . . . . . . . . . . . . 66
Kirwan-Taylor, Peter . . . . . . . . . . . . . . . . . . 58
Knudsen, 'Bunkie' . . . . . . . . . . . . . . . . . . . . 74

Lampredi, Aurelio . . . . . . . . . . . . . . . . . . . . 34
Loewy, Raymond . . . . . . . . . . . . . . . . . . 28, 82
Lord, Leonard . . . . . . . . . . . . . . . . . . . . . . . 18
Lyons, Sir William . . . . . . . . . . . . . . . . . 46, 50

Marazzi, Carrozzeria . . . . . . . . . . . . . . . . . . 52
Marek, Tadek . . . . . . . . . . . . . . . . . . . . . . . . 14
Michelotti Carrozzeria . . . . . . . . . . . . . . . . . 88
Moss, Stirling . . . . . . . . . . . . . . . . . . . . . . . . 46
Nuffield, Lord . . . . . . . . . . . . . . . . . . . . 18, 66

Olley, Maurice . . . . . . . . . . . . . . . . . . . . . . . 26

Park Ward . . . . . . . . . . . . . . . . . . . . . . . . . . . 20
Pininfarina, Carrozzeria . . . 10, 20, 32, 34, 36, 38

Rolls-Royce . . . . . . . . . . . . . . . . . . . . . . . . . . 20

Sayer, Malcolm . . . . . . . . . . . . . . . . . . . . . . . 48
Scaglietti Carrozzeria . . . . . . . . . . . . . . . 34, 36
Shelby, Carroll . . . . . . . . . . . . . . . . . . . . 8, 44
Stanzani, Paolo . . . . . . . . . . . . . . . . . . . . . . . 52
Sleator, Walter . . . . . . . . . . . . . . . . . . . . . . . 20

Tojeiro, John . . . . . . . . . . . . . . . . . . . . . . . . . 8
Touring, Carrozzeria . . . . . . . 12, 14, 16, 52, 62
Towns, William . . . . . . . . . . . . . . . . . . . . . . . 16

van Vooren . . . . . . . . . . . . . . . . . . . . . . . . . . 20
Vignale, Carrozzeria . . . . . . . . . . . . . . . . . . . 62

Wallace, Bob . . . . . . . . . . . . . . . . . . . . . . . . . 52

Yamaha Motor Co . . . . . . . . . . . . . . . . . 72, 86

Zagato, Carrozzeria . . . . . . . . . . . 10, 14, 16, 56

96